THE SACRAMENTAL SYSTEM

THE BISHOP PADDOCK LECTURES, *1892*

THE SACRAMENTAL SYSTEM

CONSIDERED AS

THE EXTENSION OF THE INCARNATION

BY

MORGAN DIX, S.T.D., D.C.L.

RECTOR OF TRINITY CHURCH, NEW YORK

WIPF & STOCK · Eugene, Oregon

Wipf and Stock Publishers
199 W 8th Ave, Suite 3
Eugene, OR 97401

The Sacramental System
Considered as the Extension of the Incarnation:
The Bishop Paddock Lectures 1892
By Dix, Morgan
Softcover ISBN-13: 978-1-6667-3438-6
Hardcover ISBN-13: 978-1-6667-9017-7
eBook ISBN-13: 978-1-6667-9018-4
Publication date 8/23/2021
Previously published by Longmans, Green, and Co., 1893

This edition is a scanned facsimile of
the original edition published in 1893.

THE BISHOP PADDOCK LECTURES.

IN the summer of the year 1880, George A. Jarvis, of Brooklyn, N. Y., moved by his sense of the great good which might thereby accrue to the cause of Christ, and to the Church of which he was an ever-grateful member, gave to the General Theological Seminary of the Protestant Episcopal Church certain securities, exceeding in value eleven thousand dollars, for the foundation and maintenance of a Lectureship in said seminary.

Out of love to a former pastor and enduring friend, the Right Rev. Benjamin Henry Paddock, D.D., Bishop of Massachusetts, he named the foundation " THE BISHOP PADDOCK LECTURESHIP."

The deed of trust declares that " *The subjects* of the lectures shall be such as appertain to the defence of the religion of Jesus Christ, as revealed in the *Holy Bible*, and illustrated in the *Book of Common Prayer*, against the varying errors of the day, whether materialistic, rationalistic, or professedly religious, and also to its defence and confirmation in respect of such central truths as the *Trinity*, the *Atonement*, *Justification*, and the *Inspiration of the Word of God,* and of such central facts as the *Church's Divine Order and Sacraments*, her historical *Reformation*, and her rights and powers as a pure and national Church. *And* other subjects may be chosen if unanimously approved by the Board of Appointment as being both timely and also within the true intent of this Lectureship."

Under the appointment of the Board created by the trust, the Rev. Morgan Dix, S.T.D., D.C.L., delivered the Lectures for the year 1892, contained in this volume.

ANALYSIS.

LECTURE I.

The Basis of the Sacramental System.

I —INTRODUCTORY   PAGE
   1. How the Subject of these Lectures was Suggested, ... 3–5
   2 Two Mysteries in the Order of Nature and in the Order of Grace, . . . 5
   3 Their Close Relation to each Other, . 6

II —ORIGIN OF THE PHRASE, "EXTENSION OF THE INCARNATION," 7

III —SACRAMENTAL DOCTRINE COEXTENSIVE WITH HISTORIC CHRISTIANITY, . . 8
   1 Witnesses to this Point
     (a) The Fathers, ... 8
     (b) Luther, and the Augsburg and Westminster Confessions, ... 8
   2. Its Basis must be sought in the Constitution of Things, ... 9
   3. Its Practical and Ideal Sides, . . 10
   4 Its Relations to Man and Nature, . 11

	PAGE
IV.—THE NATURAL WORLD ITS MYSTERY,	12
1. EXPLANATIONS:	
(a) Manichean theory,	12
(b) Pantheistic theory,	13
(c) Transcendental notions,	13
(d) Catholic teaching,	13
2. MATERIALISM	
(a) Twin brother of atheism,	14
(b) And yet rendering efficient service to the truth,	14
3. CARDINAL PRINCIPLES OF CATHOLIC DOCTRINE CONCERNING THE ORIGIN OF THE UNIVERSE,	15
4. RECENT SCIENTIFIC DISCOVERIES HAVE NOT IMPAIRED THE FORCE OF THE EVIDENTIAL ARGUMENT,	16, 17
V.—PLACE OF MAN IN THE UNIVERSE,	18
Statement of St. Thomas on this point,	19
VI.—GOD, IN THE INCARNATION, TAKES HIS PLACE, AS MAN, IN HIS OWN UNIVERSE,	20
(a) Christ the *mundi summa et compendium*,	20
(b) Catholic doctrine of the Incarnation,	21
VII.—REMEDIAL AND RESTORATIVE EFFECT OF THE INCARNATION IN NATURE,	22
(a) Exposition of Romans, viii 19–23,	23, 24
(b) Relation of Christ as Man to Creation,	25
(c) Reciprocal relation of Nature to Christ,	26
(d) Interchange of aid and help,	27

	PAGE
VIII.—EXTENT OF THE BENEFITS OF THE INCARNATION,	28
(*a*) As wide as the universe itself,	29
(*b*) Brotherhood of man, and of Christ as man, with the lower creation,	30
(*c*) Consequent explanation of the influence exerted on men by natural phenomena,	31

IX.—TWO FINAL CONSIDERATIONS

1. THE PERMANENCE OF THE BODY OF MAN, AND OF MAN IN THE BODY, ... 32, 33
    (*a*) Pagan and Christian ideas on this point contrasted, ... 34
2. THE FINAL RESTORATION OF THE HEAVENS AND THE EARTH, ... 35
    (*a*) Scriptural predictions, ... 36
    (*b*) Views of fathers and theologians, . . 37–39

LECTURE II.

The Sacramental System Coextensive with the Life and Experience of Mankind.

I.—DESIGN OF THE PRECEDING LECTURE TO SHOW THE REAL BASIS OF THE SACRAMENTAL SYSTEM, ... 43
 (*a*) No valid objection that it is hard to see and describe, ... 44
 (*b*) Every edifice must stand on a basis, . . 44
 (*c*) But the footings are not made to be seen, . 44
 (*d*) The way now open to view the superstructure, ... 45

	PAGE
II.—POPULAR HOSTILITY TO SACRAMENTAL DOCTRINE,	46
(a) Not to be treated as a transient prejudice,	47
(b) But the result of confidence in philosophic idealism and exaggerated spiritualism,	48
(c) Tendency and consequences,	49
(d) The sole remedy is the acceptance of the teachings of the Catholic religion on the Incarnation, and the bonds between God, man, and nature, in Christ,	50
III.—TRANSITION TO THE SUPERSTRUCTURE,	52
(a) Catholic theology has many sides,	53
(b) The practical and commonplace side of the subject,	53
IV.—USE OF THE WORD "SIGN" IN ANGLICAN THEOLOGY,	54
(a) Definition in the catechism,	54
(b) The use of signs coextensive with the visible creation,	55
(c) And all signs are sacramental in their character,	55
V.—THE UNIVERSE A SYSTEM OF SIGNS AND SACRAMENTS.	
(a) Visible forms and invisible life,	56
(b) Impossible to tell what life is,	56
(c) Canon Mason's statement,	57, 58
(d) Admission of Darwin,	59
(e) Life a profound mystery, and the world a sign-system all through,	59

		PAGE
VI.—MAN AN INSTANCE,		60
(a) Body, soul, and spirit,		60
(b) His existence sacramental,		61
(c) Daily meals sacramental,		61
(d) The alphabet, books, commercial paper, instances of sign-system,		61
(e) Conclusions as to life of the soul,		62
VII.—GOD MAKES HIMSELF KNOWN, NOT DIRECTLY, BUT BY SIGNS,		63
(a) Jesus Christ the crowning illustration of the sacramental principle,		63
(b) He was made man, that man might know God,		64
(c) God in Christ the sacrament of all sacraments,		65
VIII.—FURTHER ILLUSTRATIONS OF THE SUBJECT		
(a) Man in the body cannot be reached but through the body,		66
(b) Philological considerations, the classical use of the word "*sacramentum*,"		66
(c) Sacraments regarded as seals, pledges, and witnesses,		67
IX.—RECAPITULATION OF LECTURES I AND II,		68
X.—BREADTH AND GRANDEUR OF THE SACRAMENTAL SYSTEM,		69
(a) Contrast with the narrowness and poverty of modern thought,		70
(b) Those who style themselves broad are really the narrow,		71

	PAGE
XI.—ZWINGLIANISM THE IMPLACABLE FOE OF SACRAMENTAL DOCTRINE, . . .	72
(a) It has no place in our church formularies, .	72
(b) Confirmation of the statement from sundry sources, ...	72
(c) Our Offices, Articles, and system absolutely irreconcilable with Zwinglian principles, .	73

LECTURE III.

The Lesser Sacraments.

I.—NUMBER OF THE SACRAMENTS, . . .	79
(a) Latins and Eastern Churches, . . .	79
(b) Augsburg, Luther, Cranmer, .	79
(c) Article XXV, ...	80
(d) View held in ancient time, ...	81
II.—POSITION OF ANGLICAN CHURCH	
(a) Two great sacraments, ...	82
(b) Other rites of the same class, though inferior in grade, ...	83
III.—CONFIRMATION	
(a) A "following of the apostles," but not a corrupt one, ...	84
(b) Low notion of it held by many, . . .	84
(c) But really a sacramental ordinance, . .	85
(d) And rightly called a minor sacrament, .	86
IV.—HOLY MATRIMONY.	
(a) How described in Prayer-book, . .	87
(b) Called a sacrament in the Homily, . .	87
(c) Low popular ideas about it, . .	88
(d) A holy mystery in the Church, .	89

V.—HOLY ORDER.

(a) Question of the ministry a burning one to-day, ... 90
(b) Not all ministries valid, . . 91
(c) The grace of Ordination; true import of the Ordinal, . . 91

VI.—ABSOLUTION.

1   (a) By what names known, . . 92
    (b) Power of the priest to forgive sins, . 92
    (c) Confession implied in this, . . . 93

2   CHRIST FORGAVE SINS AS THE SON OF MAN.

    (a) Analysis of St Mark, ii 3-12, . . . 94
    (b) Christ's power given by Him to His ministry, 95
    (c) Words of the Ordinal, ... 95

3   TESTIMONY TO THE TEACHING OF THE CHURCH

    (a) Gray's tract on "Confession," . . . 96
    (b) Pusey's translation of Gaume, . . 97
    (c) Statement in 1st Book of Edward VI, . 99, 100
    (d) Liddon, Mahan, Ewer, ... 101, 102

VII.—UNCTION

(a) Bishop Harold Browne quoted, . . 103
(b) Bishop Forbes of Brechin, . . 104
(c) Anglican offices for unction, . . . 105
(d) Concordat with Scottish Church, . . . 105

VIII.—SUMMARY.

1. THE POSITION OF OUR CHURCH WISE AND REVERENT, ... 106

  (a) Number of sacraments not to be precisely stated or limited, ... 106
  (b) Because the whole Gospel system is sacramental, . . 107

		PAGE

2. GREAT IMPORTANCE OF THE SUBJECT, . . 108
    (*a*) The battle of the day is between Christianity and Paganism, ... 108
    (*b*) Sacraments and the supernatural go together, . . . 109–112
    (*c*) Application of the principle to every stage of human life and all the experiences of the soul, ... 112

LECTURE IV.

Holy Baptism.

I.—THE OXFORD MOVEMENT
    (*a*) Its original aim, ... 115
    (*b*) Stress laid on the doctrine of sacramental grace, ... 115
    (*c*) Dr Pusey's tract on "Baptism," . . . 116

II.—HOLY BAPTISM NECESSARY TO SALVATION
    (*a*) Scripture statements, . . . 116
    (*b*) Opposition to the doctrine of the Church, 117
    (*c*) Permanence of the Pelagian heresy, . . 118
    (*d*) Christo-Pantheism a popular fad of the day, 118

III.—THREE GIFTS IN BAPTISM.
  1. FORGIVENESS OF SINS, ... 119
    (*a*) Doctrine of the Church on original sin, . 120
    (*b*) Most easily dealt with in infancy, because no bar can then be opposed, . . 121
    (*c*) Church teaching refutes the error of those who make little or no account of sin, . 122

2 REGENERATION

    (*a*) Gorham case, ultimately a blessing, . 123
    (*b*) Pusey's definition of regeneration, . . 124
    (*c*) Man passive in the new birth, it is God's work exclusively, . 125
    (*d*) Not to be confused with change of heart, 126
    (*e*) Church teachings in accord with and supported by science, ... 128
    (*f*) Direct connection with the doctrine of the Incarnation, ... 129

3 ILLUMINATION

    (*a*) Statements in Epistle to the Hebrews, . 131
    (*b*) Light, and the organ of sight, not the same, 132
    (*c*) Material, intellectual, and spiritual light and sight, ... 133
    (*d*) Parallels and analogies, ... 134
    (*e*) Light given to the spirit in baptism, . 134
    (*f*) Whereby to see divine truth, 134
    (*g*) And constituting a new spiritual sense in us, ... 135

IV.—THE HALLOWING OF THE FONT, . 136

    (*a*) Sanctifying water to the washing away of sin, ... 136
    (*b*) Scriptural and historic review, . . 137
    (*c*) Constant occurrence of the phrase in the old liturgies and offices of the Church, . . 138
    (*d*) Tradition inviolably preserved among us, 139

V.—BEARING OF THE DOCTRINE OF HOLY BAPTISM ON THREE NOTABLE ERRORS, 140, 141

    (*a*) Remission of sin, a witness against Pelagianism, ... 140, 141

	PAGE
(*b*) Regeneration, a witness against neo-Pantheism, ...	140, 141
(*c*) Illumination, a witness against rationalistic philosophy, ...	140, 141
(*d*) Need of reassertion of Church doctrine at the present time, ...	142

LECTURE V.

Holy Communion.

I.—DEEP IMPORTANCE OF THE SUBJECT, . .	147
(*a*) Exact illustration of the sacramental extension of the Incarnation, . .	147
(*b*) Unreality of modern religion a Nemesis on the denial of the Real Presence, . .	148
II.—THE SACRAMENT OF THE ALTAR SUMS UP AND REFLECTS ALL TRUTH, . .	149
(*a*) Twofold aspect — sacrifice and sacrament, .	149
(*b*) Christ present, ...	149
(*c*) The presence effected, not by our act, but by the power of the Holy Ghost, . .	150
III.—ANALYSIS OF STATEMENTS IN THE CATECHISM, ...	151
1 RADICAL DIFFERENCE IN THE DESCRIPTION OF THE TWO SACRAMENTS, . . .	151
2. THREE TERMS TO BE CONSIDERED, . .	152
(*a*) *Signum*	
(*b*) *Res*	
(*c*) *Virtus*	
3. THESE TO BE KEPT DISTINCT, . . .	153

ANALYSIS

	PAGE
IV.—PARALLEL BETWEEN DOCTRINE OF THE INCARNATION AND THAT OF THE SACRAMENT OF THE ALTAR,	154
1. Hooker's Analysis of the Four Heresies and the Four General Councils,	154
2. Paraphrase of the said Analysis, Showing Four great Errors as to the Holy Sacrament,	155, 156

V.—THE REAL PRESENCE.

1. STATEMENT OF THE DOCTRINE, ... 157
2. IMPUGNED BY
   - (a) Transubstantiation, ... 157
   - (b) Consubstantiation, ... 157
   - (c) Virtualism, ... 157
   - (d) The sign theory, ... 157

VI.—TRANSUBSTANTIATION

- (a) Article XXVIII, ... 158
- (b) Truth of the *Signum* denied, . . . 158
- (c) Double appeal to antiquity, . . . 159
- (d) Permanence of the substance, . . . 160
- (e) And yet changed for their supernatural use, 160

VII.—ZWINGLIANISM.

- (a) Theory of memorial feast, . . 161
- (b) Repudiated by our Church, and not to be reconciled with her offices and formularies, 162
- (c) Disapproved by Protestant divines, . . 163
- (d) True place of Zwinglius, ... 163

VIII.—VIRTUALISM.

- (a) Higher teaching than that of Zwinglius, . 164

		PAGE
(b) Yet defective as denying the truth and presence of the *Res*,		165
(c) Therefore correctly described as the theory of the Real Absence,		166
(d) Strength and weakness of virtualism,		167

IX.—CONSUBSTANTIATION

    (a) Doubtful whether ever held, ... 167
    (b) Blasphemous and absurd, ... 167
    (c) And therefore not to be imputed to any one until he says that it is his belief, . . 167

X.—SUMMARY, . . . 168, 169

XI.—BRIEF REFERENCE TO THE HOLY EUCHARIST CONSIDERED AS A SACRIFICE, . 170

    Reason for not enlarging on this point, . . 171

XII.—THE DOCTRINE OF THE REAL, OBJECTIVE PRESENCE AS HELD IN THE CHURCH AN EIRENICON, ... 173–177

LECTURE VI.

The Outward Glory and the Inward Grace.

I.—TWOFOLD MANIFESTATION OF THE SACRAMENTAL SYSTEM,

    (a) Externally in Christian Worship, . . 181
    (b) Internally in believing men, . . . 181

	PAGE
II.—RITUAL OF THE CATHOLIC CHURCH,	182
(*a*) Comprehensiveness of the term,	182
(*b*) Permanence,	182
(*c*) Efforts at recovery where lost,	183
III.—SACRAMENTALITY,	184
(*a*) John Mason Neale's use of the term,	184
(*b*) Necessity of outward signs to express the idea of worship,	185
IV.—RITUAL SANCTIONED BY GOD.	
(*a*) Temple worship,	186
(*b*) Expanding into that of the Church,	186
(*c*) Iconoclasm attests the importance of the subject,	187
V.—USE OF SYMBOLISM,	188
(*a*) Absolutely necessary,	188
(*b*) Coeval with the human race,	189
(*c*) Value of the Symbol,	190, 191
VI.—CORRESPONDENCE BETWEEN THE WORSHIP OF THE CHURCH AND THE WORSHIP OFFERED BY NATURE	
(*a*) Divine worship should be beautiful and rich in form,	192
(*b*) Nature's contributions to it,	193, 194
(*c*) Logical result of denial of these principles,	195, 196
(*d*) Sceptical objection answered,	197
VII.—PRIMITIVE CHRISTIAN WORSHIP,	198
(*a*) Symbolical,	198
(*b*) Pictorial,	199
(*c*) Culmination in cathedral idea,	199

	PAGE

VIII.—DESCRIPTION OF CATHEDRAL WORSHIP,
    200, 201
    (*a*) Comment on Bryant's "Thanatopsis," . 202
    (*b*) Descent from Catholic ideas, slow but sure, to dulness and silence, . . . 203
    (*c*) Worship of Positivism as described by Malloch, ... 204, 205

IX —REVIVAL OF CATHOLIC LITURGICAL USE.
    (*a*) John Mason Neale's prediction fulfilled, . 206
    (*b*) Danger attending the movement, . . 207
    (*c*) Ritual without doctrinal signification worthless and pernicious, ... 208

X —SACRAMENTAL SYSTEM MANIFESTED IN THE LIFE OF THE SOUL, . . . 208
    (*a*) Christ the original and perfect type, . . 209
    (*b*) Imitation of Him impresses a distinct character on soul and body of man, . . . 210

XI —CONCLUSION, ... 211–214

I.

BASIS OF THE SACRAMENTAL SYSTEM.

LECTURE I.

THE BASIS OF THE SACRAMENTAL SYSTEM.

ON a Saturday afternoon, in the midsummer of last year, I found myself by chance on the southern shore of Otsego Lake, looking northward on a scene which for quiet and soothing beauty can hardly be surpassed. Before me lay the mirror of the Glimmerglass; warm lights threw a flush upon the skies; the day was going away; the omens of the evening were already in the clouds; a breeze, scarcely strong enough to ruffle the water, came from the western hills; the woods were reflected in their native colors along the silent shore. But below was more than what met the eye. Through and under this exterior beauty, voices could be heard, speaking of the mystery of the natural world. It has been said of the study of nature, "that it is hardly profane to characterize it as a means of grace to man." *

---

* See an article in *Garden and Forest*, August 12, 1891.

The words are words of truth, in nature is a tonic for mind and heart. Here are depths which no man has yet sounded, not philosopher nor poet; here is a mystery which thus far defies our search—whence, and how, came this wondrous, beautiful world, *when* it was made; and *why* it was made "subject to vanity;" how long, before man appeared on the earth, his destiny and doom were foreshadowed there; how he, in his fortunes, is linked to what he calls "nature"; by what bond and to what extent it is so related to him as to sympathize with him in his sorrows, and partake of his hope—what poet, what philosopher, what theologian has told us the whole truth on these points? Of them might one readily be led to muse, while looking upon the lake, confronted by forests and hills, and the perspective of point, bluff, and mountain; for at such times and in such places men become aware of some unspeakable strangeness in their life, and, keeping silence before mysterious and dimly indicated presences, they know that it must be possible to draw its hidden meaning from God's world, from hill and plain, from deep, still waters and shadowy woods, from the currents of the evening breeze and the outstretched shadows of ebbing day.

Hard by that lake stands an old church, shaded by tall pines and other trees, and keeping watch and ward over the surrounding resting-places of the dead in Christ. On the following morning I found myself at the early celebration in that venerable fane. Here another mystery confronted us, like the other, too deep to search out; the mystery of the Coming of our Lord, in Holy Communion. The church also, like the lake, was held in the stillness of a holy peace. The voice of the priest, as he recited the office, was the only sound that broke upon the ear; the words of Christ were repeated; and then, to the eye of faith, "came Jesus and stood in the midst, and said, Peace be unto you" Both the mysteries of which I have been speaking were of God, one in the order of nature, the other in the order of grace. And at that time it occurred to me—remembering an accepted invitation to speak to you on some sacred theme—that the subject had been assigned, on the shore of the lake in the evening, and in the church in that consecrated morning hour. Is there not a parallelism, a correlation, between these two mysteries? May there not be, to other, larger eyes than ours, points at which they touch or interpenetrate? May not the mystery in nature pass onward and upward to the mystery in grace? And may not the mystery in grace be more deeply felt when interpreted by the mystery in nature? Can this be, that the natural world holds some relation to man in his life, which is realized to him in that profoundest of all wonders, the Sacrament of the Altar? May not the same Hand which beckons to us through the veil of nature be laid upon us to bless as we kneel in adoration before "those holy mysteries"? The inspired writers ascribe personality to tree and mountain and hill, calling on them to clap their hands, to sing, to show forth God's praise. Our own poets represent the inanimate world as if it had voices and a mission to men. Is this mere metaphor? Is there no truth in it? The light natural and the light supernatural; the beauty of the material world and the beauty of the Kingdom of Heaven: come they not both of God? And are there not relationships between them more intimate than we suppose, too subtile for us to comprehend? On that line would I lead you this evening, as we think of the treasures of our inheritance in the holy Church of Jesus Christ.

It is a high honor and privilege to lecture before this Seminary. The series delivered on this

"Bishop Paddock Foundation" a year ago had for its subject the Incarnation. I propose, as my theme this year, the Sacramental System. There is, I trust, a fitness in this order. "The fathers," says Bishop Jeremy Taylor, "by an elegant expression, call the blessed sacrament the extension of the incarnation." The idea was, no doubt, derived by them from what St. Paul said about those "joints and bands" by which grace is ministered to us, and through which the whole body "increaseth with the increase of God." (Col. iii. 19; Eph. iv. 16.) And so, in accord with "Holy Scripture, and Ancient Authors," our own Richard Hooker, in the fifth book of the Ecclesiastical Polity, lays the foundation of his teaching on the holy sacraments in that full, minute, and incomparable statement of the Catholic doctrine of the Incarnation, with which you are no doubt familiar. To follow up the lectures of last year on the Incarnation by a course on the Sacraments seems, therefore, in order; and to this, in reliance on divine aid, I now proceed.

Of sacramental doctrine this may be truly said, that it is coextensive with historic Christianity. Of this there is no reasonable doubt, as regards the very ancient days, of which St. Chrysostom's treatise on the priesthood and St. Cyril's catechetical lectures may be taken as characteristic documents. Nor was it otherwise with the more conservative of the reformed bodies in the sixteenth century. Martin Luther's catechism, the Augsburg, and later the Westminster, confessions are strongly sacramental in their tone, putting to shame the degenerate followers of the men who compiled them. What is the basis of a system obviously coextensive with Christianity? There are those who, while holding sacramental doctrine, take their starting-point in a correspondence with the twofold constitution of man's nature, a congruity with the practical experience of our everyday life. But surely there is a point of departure much more remote than these; we may go beyond the lower range of simile, fitness, and happy adaptation to circumstances, and trace its origin far back of such obvious considerations. Nay, it were well to do so, in the interests of humanity, for who can tell how many objectors would be silenced, how many unhappy doubters convinced, could they but see the subject in its fulness and depth?

The Sacramental System claims, even on philosophical grounds, the attention of the closest students of nature and the best thinkers of the age;

and where it is lightly esteemed, the reason may be that it has been presented in a dry and lifeless way, and commended to regard on no higher grounds than those of expediency or convenience; so that it offers nothing to touch the soul, excite the imagination, or challenge faith. The Sacramental System has been given away in exchange for the lucubrations of rationalism, or degraded to the level of empty ceremonies, bald signs, and forms without life. To quote from Robert Isaac Wilberforce, referring to the low and partial estimate of sacraments:

"It rests their use on our act only, not on that of God, it is merely subjective, human, tentative, and though useful as a direction to ourselves, falls far short of the sublime views which Scripture opens respecting these 'holy mysteries' It is a conception such as a Socinian might entertain, but with which the Christian mind could never be satisfied "*

Far different is the Sacramental System when presented to devout consideration as included in the eternal purpose of God; effectuated through an alliance between God and His material, moral,

---

* "Doctrine of the Incarnation," ch. xiii. p 405

and spiritual creation; having relations of some kind to all the kingdoms of nature, and probably extending in its influence beyond the limits of the terrestrial sphere.

The system which we are about to consider has two sides, a practical and almost commonplace side, and an ideal and mystical side. In the latter relation it is proposed to treat of it in this lecture. I do not intend to make an argument in logical form, but simply to present a series of considerations which seem to bear with cogency upon the subject. That nature is neither self-existing nor independent, but the work of God, and constantly ruled by God, that man is a summary of nature; that there is between the natural world and ourselves an intimate connection; that the disorders observable in the natural world have something to do with the trouble in us men, so that relief to us carries with it benefit of some sort to the world outside of us; that through the Incarnation God has Himself, in person, taken a unique place in the natural world, as man: these are the points which shall first be presented to your thoughts. And next it will be suggested, as a just inference, that in the work of repairing and reconstructing humanity, by the extension of the Incarnation to individual souls, the natural world may be drawn upon for help, and its elements put to use as instrumental means whereby that race shall be aided, in whose recovery nature herself has an interest and a direct concern. Here may be found a basis for the Sacramental System deeper than that of congruity, adaptation, or convenience. The employment of such a system is not to be regarded merely as a happy thought, a lucky hit, an appropriate idea, but it comes in because things are as they are, because nature is summed up in man; because all things work together for good to them that love God; because "the creature" itself is bound up in our fortunes, and may very fitly be employed in the process of our extrication from present evils. Such thoughts, if they prove to be true and in harmony with the Catholic faith, must place the subject beyond the reach of frivolous objection and lift it to the height which it seems, for some sufficient reason, to have held through all past ages of the Church.

Let us enter, with reverence and circumspection, a path rendered more attractive by the mysteries with which it is encompassed on the right hand and on the left. And, first, to speak of nature.

> "To him who, in the love of nature, holds
> Communion with her visible forms, she speaks
> A various language"

So sings a poet of our own land. But what, after all our study, do we know of nature? What is meant by the word? And what progress has been made in interpreting her secrets? There are two great heresies relating to the natural world; one cuts it off from Almighty God, the other confounds it substantially with Him. To some nature is a vast, godless phenomenon, the outcome of a blind movement, directed by no intelligent ruler or governor. Such persons make it a stupendous fetich; they ascribe to it personality, they talk of nature's laws and nature's designs and nature's acts as if nature were as God to us. In their anxious interest men have run into innumerable conjectures. The Manichean says that matter is essentially evil; the gnostic conceives of the natural world as the work of a malevolent demiurge, the rival and ancient foe of God. To some, as they speculate on the universe, its existence appears a necessity; God is constrained to be always a creator; He can never have been without a manifestation exterior to Himself. To the pantheist, nature and God are the same—one universal and all-pervading substance; nature is God taking form and shape; God evolving and developing; God sleeping in the rock, moving in the lower creation, coming to thought and self-knowledge in man. The transcendentalist runs into unintelligible talk, telling us that "Nature is the incarnation of a thought, and turns to a thought again, as ice becomes water and gas; that the world is mind precipitated, and that the volatile essence is forever escaping again into the state of free thought."* Such are instances of the efforts of man to get at the secret of "the rounded world, nine times folded in mystery." But a Catholic Christian is protected by his faith from such erroneous and wild opinions; he does not know all; he does not pretend to know much; but he knows something, and what he knows is worth knowing. To him nature is not a self-existing phenomenon, nor the result of chance, nor yet

"A hollow form with empty hands."

In the creed of the Catholic Church he has light on this subject; that light comes in the sublime declaration of the existence of "One God the Father Almighty, Maker of heaven and earth, and of all things visible and invisible," it comes in the

---

* See Emerson's essay on "Nature."

further statement that God, having created the heavens and the earth, "saw everything that He had made, and behold, it was very good." * Here, at all events, are starting-points; lines on which to move with some confidence in our study of the mystery; first principles to save us from the blank hollowness of intuitive religionism and the unintelligible utterances of the ideal philosopher. Even the materialist renders us a not unimportant service at this point of our studies. Of dogmatic materialism it has been well said, that

> "It is the twin brother of atheism. It may well be called the gospel of the flesh; it is the absolute deification of matter and of the creature. The materialists are the most dangerous enemies of progress that the world has ever seen"†

The charge is true of materialism, as a philosophic system pretending to explain all, and to account for man in his entire state. But materialism has its uses and serves a good purpose to the Catholic faith. As Dr. Liddon remarks:

> "Materialism has done valuable service in correcting the exaggeration of a one-sided spiritualism. It is common but erroneous to speak of man's body as being related to his

---

* Gen. i. 31.
† Christlieb, "Modern Doubt and Christian Belief," Lecture III. ii.

spirit only as is the casket to the jewel which it contains. But, as a matter of fact, the personal spirit of man strikes its roots far and deep into the encompassing frame of sense, with which, from the first moment of its existence, it has been so intimately associated. The spirit can indeed exist independently of the body, but this independent existence is not its emancipation from a prison-house of matter and sense, it is a temporary and abnormal divorce from the companion whose presence is needed to complete its life"

The mystery of creation is not to be solved by the materialist, the pantheist, the transcendentalist, or the ideal philosopher. In their methods they confuse matter and mind; they sacrifice the flesh to the spirit or the spirit to the flesh; they confound the Creator and the creature; they let go the real to chase a phantom; they deny the evidence of the senses or the facts of human experience. There is no escape from their errors save in the acceptance of these cardinal principles of Catholic doctrine:

(*a*) That God alone is uncreate and eternal.

(*b*) That He made all things by the word of His power, not of His own substance, but of elements created by Him for their purpose.

(*c*) That He made all things good.

(*d*) That He rules and governs all.

These statements constitute the formal contradiction of gnostic, Manichean, and pantheistic errors, and of materialistic and idealistic speculations. They begin by asserting the essential distinction between God and nature, the supernatural order and the visible universe, the material and intelligent creations. They affirm that matter, the physical basis of all visible things, is God's handiwork; that it is essentially good and not evil; that the world came into being through Him; that it was the product of His wisdom and love; that it deserves our reverent study as a manifestation of the divine Creator; and that by study of the wonders of the universe we can come to the knowledge of ourselves and God.

And here let me remark, in passing, on the failure of recent attempts to discredit the evidential argument from nature in proof of the truths of religion. What St. Paul said nearly nineteen hundred years ago is as true to-day as then, that the invisible things of God may be understood by the things that are made, even His eternal power and godhead.* Against the denial of this fact, based on supposed scientific discoveries, a reaction has already set in; it is admitted that those discoveries,

---

* Rom 1 20

instead of weakening, have strengthened that branch of the evidences of natural religion. God is more clearly revealed in His intelligence, power, and love, the more closely we study His works. To quote Mr. Gore, in his recently published "Bampton Lectures:"

"If Charles Darwin and the scientific world whom he represents have materially altered, yet they have not fundamentally impaired the evidences in nature of divine purpose or design, nor have they touched the argument (to many minds the irresistible argument) from the beauty of nature to the spirituality of the Being which it reveals."—Lecture II

Creation is the work of an almighty and benevolent God; a mirror which reveals Him. As we look into that mirror we are held to it by a strange fascination. What is the secret of that fascination? It arises, unquestionably, from the perception of a relationship between nature and ourselves. What is the place of man in the universe of wonders? Let us proceed to consider this point.

It is a striking remark of Emerson, that "the roots of all things are in Man." To Catholics this is a familiar thought. It is said that man, in his progress from obscure embryonic rudiments to the state in which he emerges from the womb into the outer world, passes through many a stage of lower life. And nowhere is Catholic theology more bold or more masterful than in its account of man in this relation to the universe. Let us hear the words of a great teacher on this point:

"God, in creating the heavens and the earth, created two worlds in one a world invisible and celestial, the city of spirits, and a world terrestrial and visible, the country of material bodies Until man appeared on the earth, there were sensitive life and vegetative life, but there was no intelligent life . In creating man, God joined together spirit and body in the unity of a single being, in such a way that the being of the soul is also the being of the body, and in consequence, in this marvellous creature, the spirit has a corporal being and a corporal life, while the body receives a spiritual being and a spiritual life, the intelligence has, as it were, a material personality, while the material is elevated to a species of intelligent personality, so that in man we find this material body of ours speaking and acting as the spirit speaks and acts, to which the lower is united substantially without confusion Matter and body are associated with spirit in man, for the worship of God and for the service of religion "*

This is man; the *minor mundus*, as he has been called; matter and spirit in one person; represent-

---

* "La Raison Philosophique et la Raison Catholique · Conferences by Father Ventura de Ravlica " Paris, Gaume Freres, 1854

ing and including two worlds; having the entire created universe summed up in him. According to St. Thomas Aquinas:

> "Man is not only in touch with the intellectual order by way of his intelligence, and with the material order through his senses, but also, being both spirit and body, he is in himself a summary of the conditions of all bodies and of all spirits Like God, he is independent of every other created being, he is intelligent, like the angels, and at the same time he has the sensitive life of the brute, the vegetative life of the plant, the augmentative life of the mineral, the inert existence of inorganic beings, and thus, uniting in himself the elements of all beings, the forces of all lives in creation, he produces all the effects thereof and embraces all its harmonies; he is, in short, the world in small, the summary, the abridgment of the world, '*mundi summa et compendium*'"

Such is man, and this is his place in the universe. And here we come to that stupendous fact in the history of creation which consigns to relative insignificance the questions so much discussed, about the mode of creation, the age of the world, protoplasm, evolution, and the like. The fact referred to is that of the Incarnation. The Creator has come into His own universe, and has taken it bodily ($\sigma\omega\mu\alpha\tau\iota\varkappa\tilde{\omega}\varsigma$)* into Himself, in assuming

---

* Col ii 9

our humanity. We assert, as Catholics, while repudiating pantheistic ideas of consubstantiation, commingling, or identification, that God, the personal Creator, by whom all things were made and do consist, was pleased to unite and join together in His person two natures, absolutely diverse and distinct; and that, of these two, one was substantially a summary of the created universe. "*Homo factus est.*" You know that it was human nature, and not a human person, through which the Incarnation was effected. Jesus Christ was not an individual of our race, one in number of Adam's line, born in the natural order, and, subsequently to such birth, united to God. That would not have been incarnation at all in the Catholic sense of the word But a nature, and not a person, was joined to the Godhead, $\dot{a}\lambda\eta\theta\tilde{\omega}s$, $\tau\varepsilon\lambda\dot{\varepsilon}\omega s$, $a\delta\iota a\iota\rho\dot{\varepsilon}\tau\omega s$, $a\sigma\upsilon\gamma\chi\upsilon\tau\dot{\omega}s$. And therefore, whatever relation man sustains towards the other orders of creation and the kingdoms of nature, the same does Christ, as man, sustain to them. He, being perfect man, is related to the visible and material creation as truly as to the intellectual and spiritual world. He also may be called the microcosm, the *minor mundus, mundi summa et compendium*. And to think of Christ as now an abstract and incorporeal spiritual essence would be the same error as to strike out the body from the description of a man, and to represent him as essentially like to the angels.

In the Catholic doctrine this relation of the world to God and of God to the world is presented to our faith. To say that one man of our race, born after the manner common to us all, was taken up into unity with God, would be to throw away a glorious truth, and drop to a lame and impotent conclusion. If Jesus Christ had been the son of Joseph and Mary, whatever might have been done for Him at any period of His life would have affected Him and Him only. There is an element of the ludicrous and fantastical in the idea of such an exaltation and glorifying of one particular man out of all that ever lived, for no assignable reason unless "*pour encourager les autres;*" nor could we, on such a poverty-stricken hypothesis, come to that magnificent conception of the alliance between the universe and its Creator. Not to one human person, not to one exceptionally favored individual of Adam's line, not to a man like Moses or Gautama or Socrates, were divine honor and the dignity of exaltation to equality with God awarded. What God assumed was human nature, and not a human person. He who is ever with His creation, entered into His own world in a new way; He became man; and thus a new relationship was formed between Him and that creation which owed its existence to Him, and which, from the beginning, He had governed and controlled.

Let us advance a step. Why did God the Son become incarnate? And how far do the benefits of the Incarnation extend? In answering the first of these questions we are brought face to face with the trouble and sorrow in the world. It is unnecessary to discuss the question whether the Incarnation would have taken place, though man had not fallen; it suffices to take facts as they are, and to note that the work had a remedial and restorative effect. It applied, first, to mankind in a state of depression and decline, and secondly, to the whole creation, of which we are told that it is disastrously affected by the condition of man, its head. Let us take up, next, the statements of Holy Scripture on this mysterious subject.

The late Bishop of Edinburgh, in a work entitled "Does Science aid Faith in regard to Creation?"[*] says:

---

[*] Published by Hodder & Stoughton, London, 1883

"There is one part of the Christian faith on the subject of creation to which I think sufficient attention has never been given by theologians And, instructive as it is in itself, as connected with our faith on redemption, it has become in modern times specially important in its relation to the progress of science, and it is one in which, perhaps, more than in any other direction whatever, science has proved itself the serviceable handmaid of faith instead of being its rival and adversary I refer to the view of creation which St Paul sets forth in the eighth chapter of his Epistle to the Romans, in which chapter he brings to its climax and glorious consummation the argument which he had commenced in the fifth chapter of that epistle, as to the victory through Christ of righteousness over sin, grace over wrath and condemnation, and life over death " (p 82)

The subject, in the passage thus referred to, is the creation, in the Greek κτίσις, in the Latin *creatura*, in King James' version the *creature*, in the Revised version (and correctly), the creation. As Bishop Cotterill says: "The word is here used in its ordinary sense, and includes all the material creation, animate and inanimate; it answers as nearly as possible to '*nature*' in our modern use of the word." Now as to the κτίσις, creation, or nature, St. Paul affirms that something in it is wrong. It was "made subject to vanity," not of its own will, as in the case of Adam when he fell; but by the will of the Creator, who with a purpose, and in pursuance of a design, "subjected the same to vanity." It is the result of that subjection that "the whole creation groaneth and travaileth in pain together until now." Yet through that state of depression runs the golden thread of hope: "the earnest expectation of the creation waiteth for the manifestation of the sons of God." The universe, with which we are connected and to which, through the Incarnation, God is allied and personally united, is in trouble, in long and serious trouble, in some strange distress imposed on it in the far-off past; it is expectant; it has a hope; it is looking forward to something; it is waiting for "the redemption of our body."* Some strange, close, and intimate relationship exists between man and what he calls Nature. And this seems to be the reason why, as the Bishop of Durham has observed, the old fathers of the Church so often led their pupils to that lofty and divine and most lovely study of the visible world, and found a basis for their teachings in a rational feeling for the vast grandeur of the external order, "the sacred economy of the universe," as St. Gregory calls it † True, there is

---

* See Appended Notes, No I
† "Essays in the Religious Thought of the West." by Brooke Foss Westcott, D.D , D C L., p 215

disorder in that universe; its sacred harmonies are marred by discords; there is sorrow on land and sea, and weather casts of trouble are in the skies above us. But relief is expected; it has been promised; it shall surely come. It is coming through the redemption of our body and along with the manifestation of the sons of God. But redemption and sonship in God are gifts to man through the Incarnation of the Eternal Son; so that His work acts beyond us, and finds a field for its beneficent exercise below the circle of His intelligent creation. Christ's work cannot be limited to the human race; it cannot be exhausted in rescuing us from sin and death; there are ranges beyond where He worketh, though in ways not revealed to us; and believing this, we are brought very close to the object of our quest; we have reached the point at which we may confidently look for the basis of the Sacramental System, and find out how the material elements have been made to minister to us in our spiritual and moral life.

For, if man be the summary of creation; if Christ be truly man, and, as such, related to the material universe, through His humanity, as we are to it through ours; if the "creature" is in trouble, not through its own fault, but as if it were bearing our trouble, and subject to vanity on our account and for our sakes; if Christ is really come, and is standing in His place, summing up in His person all the power and forces of the universe, and bringing them to bear on us men for our salvation; if our rescue and redemption are helping creation already, and are to help it still more in ways not yet apparent nor fully understood; if creation be deeply interested and concerned in the "redemption of that body" by which man touches the material universe as in his intelligence he touches the spiritual realm; if all these things are so, why, we may ask, should it be deemed incredible—why might it not be expected as a matter of course—that in the work of man's redemption and deliverance some powers, some elements, of the natural order should be used as instruments for that purpose? In connection with that silent and inarticulate sympathy with man, why should not nature proffer such help as she may be able to give? Why should not Christ, the great deliverer, use the elements of this world in bringing about spiritual effects? He asserted His lordship over earth, air, fire, and water, while here; He calmed the angry sea; He made clay an instrument of opening the eyes of the blind; He scattered to the winds the powers of darkness; in

His remedial processes He drew upon the pharmacy of nature. Was this only for convenience' sake, or for the purposes of a barren symbolism? Was there a deeper meaning in it? Nature, in her normal condition, offers medicines for the healing of the body; vegetable and mineral helps, tonics, febrifuges, anodynes. Why should not the Holy Ghost, through natural elements, exalted to a supernatural efficacy, minister to the diseases of the soul? Why should not earth, air, fire, and water be made to help us? The element of water, by which three-fourths of the globe is covered, of which great part of the human body is made up, why should it not be "sanctified to the washing away of sin"? The corn, which groweth up out of the earth, and is bruised and ground in the mortar, and baked in the fire; the grape, which ripens in the sunshine; why should not these be used for spiritual purposes, as instrumental means of sanctification and holy gifts, to purify, feed, and hallow human life? What is there strained or repellent in the idea of such ministration of the natural elements to Him who, though the head and crown of nature, needs all the help that can be given from heaven and earth? The application of material agents to spiritual uses through a consecration such as the divine power knows how to effect, is not only a simple idea, it is the sequel to that act of the Eternal Son of God in assuming a mortal body and a human soul. Sacramental religion may accordingly be considered as the purest and simplest of all religions. It follows the line on which our redemption proceeds; on which the release of the creation from vanity is now proceeding.

And then comes another question: How far do the benefits of the Incarnation extend? Who can say? Who can limit the work of God the Son? Who can draw a line, and tell us how much it may take in before the end; how deeply it strikes into the frame of nature; how comprehensive it may prove, when we see the full extent of the mystery, as we shall by and by? Are there inhabitants in the spheres about us? Have they intelligence, and a moral nature? Is this earth the only orb, in the myriads and myriads of the universe, where living, thinking, speaking creatures are to be found? Sooner than be content with a narrow theory on these points, let us give the thoughts and the imagination free play; let us appropriate the language of the old Breviary hymn, in which the benefits of the atonement are boldly and thrillingly extended to all kingdoms of the earth and to other worlds than this:

> " Terra, pontus, astra, mundus,
> Quo lavantur flumine "*

Such thoughts as these, or such dreams, if you like that word better, are at all events in accord with the Catholic faith, and the mind of the Church. In proof of this statement, reference may be made to the fathers and saints, who from time to time have felt and expressed intense sympathy with nature, and even professed a sense of brotherhood with beings of the lower orders of creation. If one of the enlightened, highly cultured and eminently practical people of our own day were to be asked which of all the legends of the saints he thought the silliest, he would probably mention that of St. Anthony of Padua, who preached to the fishes, or that of St. Francis of Assisi, calling the birds of the air about him, and bidding them and other creatures unite

---

*Happily, we have this noble lyric in our new Hymnal, the lines are thus rendered ·

> " Whence, to cleanse the whole creation,
> Streams of blood and water flow "

with him in praising their Lord and ours. But is there not a truth here which we ought to discern? Is not this one application of the doctrine of St. Paul? Who knows that birds and beasts, the fowl that fly in the firmament, and all that move in the waters, may not in their own way be more religious than man? What soul so dull and cold as to find no meaning in the pleasant sounds of morning and noonday, of evening and night, while the swift earth rolls on her course, and suns and stars rise and set, and moons wax and wane, and many a plaintive voice seems chanting to God; the shrill cicada uttering its cry, and the cricket practising its cheerful song? Few pictures are more delightful than that of the holy man who so dearly loved the lower creation, and was gentle and tender to all that hath breath; whom Mrs. Jameson has charmingly described as

"wandering over those beautiful Umbrian mountains, from Assisi to Gubbio, singing with a loud voice hymns (*alla Francese*, as the old legend expresses it, whatever that may mean), and praising God for all things—for the sun which shone above, for the day and for the night, for his *mother* the earth, and for his *sister* the moon, for the winds which blew in his face, for the pure, precious water, and for the jocund fire, for the flowers under his feet, and for the stars above his head—saluting and blessing all creatures, whether animate or inanimate, as his brethren and sisters in the Lord.*

Do you ask an explanation of the influence exerted over man by the aspect and phenomena of the natural world? Find it in the fact of an intimate relationship between us and it; as, through our material constitution, part and parcel thereof; as having joint interests, and a community in pain and hope. And in that relationship find also the justification of that Sacramental System, to which such persistent objections are made where the conditions of human existence are imperfectly understood. No other system addresses us with such force; none offers so much as this. On other grounds also it makes appeal to the enlightened reason; but we shall not feel it for all that it is, till we have gone to the heart and centre of things created; to that depth and that height at which man touches the material and immaterial orders at once; until we see God taking creation, summed up in human nature, into alliance with His eternal and infinite Being, in a unity in which they are to continue and abide hence-

---

* "Legends of the Monastic Orders," p 241.

forth and forever.* In the person of the Son of God, the Godhead and Manhood were joined together, never to be divided. But man is the crown of creation; and through him God draws His own work lovingly to Himself.

I shall call your attention in the next lecture to some other aspects of the Sacramental System in which it is commended to our confidence and faith. But, in conclusion, let me speak briefly on two points which come in here, in the discussion of our subject.

Through the mortal body is established the connection between man and the material creation. But the body is an integral part of us, not less necessary to our perfection and completeness than the intelligence, the spirit, and the soul. "*Perfect man, of a reasonable soul and human flesh subsisting. . . . The reasonable soul and flesh is one man.*" † A reasonable soul without human flesh is not perfect man; a man without a body would not be a man. The permanence of the body and the flesh, accordingly, is a truth of the Catholic religion. The body is to live forever, as well as

---

* See Art. II "The Godhead and Manhood were joined together in One Person, never to be divided"
† Symbol called *Quicunque vult*

the soul; with the soul it is co-heir of immortality; and therefore, in preparation for its higher destiny, it is now the subject of refining, purifying, and restorative processes, intended to cleanse, to feed, to maintain it in strength and health, and to insure its rescue from the rude and awful shock of death. It is to be redeemed, raised up, and made (to use St. Paul's description), $ἄφθαρτον, δυνάτον, πνευματικόν$, incorruptible, powerful, glorious. The human body is not a mere shell, which the exultant spirit is to burst some day, glad to be rid of its old companion; it is not an empty sign, to disappear by and by forever; it is the permanent and necessary equipment of man as man. In the sight of a Christian the body is a sacred thing. The Holy Ghost makes it His temple; to profane it is sacrilege.* It is to be offered as a living sacrifice, holy and acceptable to God.† Man's service is, first, last, and always, a bodily service. Corporal and spiritual works of mercy go on together. Grace is given to the body, as well as to the soul; our sinful bodies are made clean by the touch of the Body of the Lord in Holy Communion. The Sacramental System accords with this conception of the place

---

* 1 Cor. vi. 19.   † Rom xii. 1.

and destiny of the human body; and wherever that system is rejected, we may expect to find conceptions and notions of our nature and our state better befitting a pagan than a Christian; perhaps a disbelief in the resurrection of that Blessed Body in which our salvation was wrought out; perhaps, if not certainly, disbelief in the resurrection of our own. Philosophic idealism, presumptuous spiritualism, are the inevitable refuge of him who misconceives the constitution of human nature, and denies to the body its place and rights.

That man, in his death, is instantly to pass into the condition of abstract and incorporeal spirit, and so to remain, glad and content, forever, is an idea which rests on no good evidence, and brings no comfort; it is little less disquieting and alarming than the thought that man must

> " . . . drop from out this universal frame,
> Into that shapeless, scopeless, blank abyss,
> That utter nothingness from which he came."*

From such terrifying dreams we are saved by faith in the Sacramental System, in its principles and application. It deals with us, not as pure spirits caged for a while in deleterious bodies, but

---

* " Dream of Gerontius "

as real and true men; it gives us credit for all that we are; it asserts the worth and dignity of the body; declares it to be a sharer with the soul in redemption; predicts its survival and future development in a higher state; draws on the material world for help; and uses as instrumental means for spiritual ends, things below the intellectual order. There is a fitness here which can hardly be denied.

By one more consideration is this view of the Sacramental System supported. In Holy Scripture, we find the positive assertion of the retention of some of those things with which we are now connected, and their continuance hereafter under new conditions and in new forms. It is a consoling and tranquillizing thought. Consider this beautiful and wonderful universe; the revealer of the glory of the Lord, the teacher, the prophet, the treasure-house of mystic symbolism, this home of wayfaring men, so dear, so pleasant; why should its doom be, like that of the wicked, complete destruction and perpetual disuse and darkness? Is there really any ground for the statement that annihilation, non-existence, is to be the end of these works of His hands? Are we not told the very reverse? Why should not nature, though full of disorder and distress, be hereafter purified, restored, and brought back to the state in which the Voice proclaimed it good? Are there not, in the Old Testament and in the New, words to that effect? The intimations are not obscure; we look for a work of reparation and renewal, as among the final purposes of the Lord. "*The earth and the works that are therein shall be burned up . . . the heavens being on fire shall be dissolved, and the elements shall melt with fervent heat.*" But is this to be the end? Nay, it says: "*We, according to his promise, look for new heavens and a new earth, wherein dwelleth righteousness.*"* Prophets of old testified to the same effect. "*Behold, I create new heavens and a new earth,*" saith the Spirit by the mouth of Isaiah.† "*And I saw new heavens and a new earth,*" responds the Evangelist, in his vision, by the same Spirit.‡ Such statements present no difficulty to a believer in the Incarnation. It seems reasonable to him, that as man is to be raised from death and made glorious, powerful, and incorruptible, so the creation of which he is the sum and crown may also arise, glorious and beautiful, out of the flames of future burnings; that this whole creation, which

---

* 2 Pet iii 10   † Isa lxv 17   ‡ Rev xxi. 1

now groaneth and travaileth in pain together, may hereafter rejoice and give thanks as when the morning stars sang together and all the sons of God shouted for joy.* The creature looketh for the redemption of the body; why, unless perceiving, through some inexplicable consciousness, that its own redemption is bound up in ours? It would not be, I think, profane to surmise, that as God is preparing mankind for life and everlasting felicity, so He may be employing other sacramental means, unknown to us, by which, in other departments of nature, a work is even now in progress, the results of which are hereafter to appear—results which may overwhelm our narrow and selfish thinkers with complete confusion.

"What is this creation?" asks St Chrysostom, in commenting on the words of St Paul. "Not thyself alone, but that also which is thy inferior, and partaketh not of reason or sense, this, too, shall be a sharer in thy blessings For it shall be freed, he says, from the bondage of corruption, that is, it shall no longer be corruptible, but shall go along with the beauty given to thy body, just as when this became corruptible that became corruptible also, so, now it is made incorruptible, that also shall follow it too . . . Thou art suffering for thyself, the creation for thee. . . . As men,

---

* Job, xxxviii 7.

when a son is to appear at his coming to a dignity, clothe even the servants with a brighter garment, to the glory of the son, so will God also clothe the creature with incorruption for the glorious liberty of the children . . ."

And, elsewhere, the father adds:

"He partially exposes to thy view the things to come, setting before thee the change of thy body, and along with it the change of the whole creation "*

It is time to bring these remarks to a close. They are mere suggestions or hints on a subject so wide and so full of wonder and mystery that a volume would hardly suffice for its full discussion. They are left to you, for reflection, before we proceed to some considerations of an inferior, but, perhaps, a more popular and practical character. Let me close what has been said thus far, by quoting the words of Godet:

"As in our present body we see the two systems, animal and vegetable, which are around us, converging, and in them nature, as it is on earth, in its entirety so will the future body be the centre of a nature renewed and glorified, freed from the law of vanity and death The ideal, after which are instinctively yearning, not men only, but, as St Paul says, *all creatures*, will be realized " †

---

* St. Chrys , Hom xiv on Rom viii 21–23.
† "Studies on the Old Testament," ii p 62.

And to these words let me add others of a doctor and teacher of our own Church, and a professor emeritus of this seminary, commending to your attention the entire passage of which they form a part :

"The work of redemption closely corresponded to that of creation, and therefore is properly a new creation, whether we regard it in its effects upon individual men, upon the whole company of the redeemed, or upon all the creation of which man was the crown It will not reach its destined end till the creation that has been darkened and ruined by sin shall be restored to its original beauty and perfection " *

---

* Professor Buel "Treatise of Dogmatic Theology," Vol I, ch. VI , of Creation and Providence see whole passage, pp 250–253

II.

THE SACRAMENTAL SYSTEM COEXTENSIVE WITH THE LIFE AND EXPERIENCE OF MANKIND.

LECTURE II

THE SACRAMENTAL SYSTEM COEXTENSIVE WITH THE LIFE AND EXPERIENCE OF MANKIND.

IN the first lecture of this course your attention was directed to what are deemed to be the real foundations of the Sacramental System. Every structure stands upon a basement of some sort; and it appeared to me that the first thing to be done, in the defence and vindication of a system so misunderstood as this, was to show that we have something to allege in its behalf more weighty than considerations of convenience or the perception of a general agreement with things in the world. The Cathedral, the Capitol, the Chambers of Justice, and whatever other edifices there be, stand on substructures; the larger the edifice, the broader spread the courses of masonry below. What shall be said of the Sacramental System, whose maker and builder is God, which is ample enough to gather in the nations; in whose successive stories, as they rise upward, room and place are provided for all people, tongues, and languages of the redeemed?

Must not a structure such as this have a foundation commensurate with its proportions and adequate to its design? That is what I have already suggested for your consideration, alleging that a system so large and grand may be regarded as undoubtedly anchored somewhere in the roots and bases of the universe itself. Nor does it make against this view of the case, that men protest their inability to see any such foundation, and challenge us to describe it accurately, and to explain how it was laid. Who sees the foundation of any building, large or small? What architects call the Footings are not seen, nor were they meant to be seen. With care and close calculation are they laid, and then they are at once hidden away; none knows exactly their dimensions or arrangement but the man who set them in their place; basement, story, and stage after stage tower up in the air, but these are not the foundations; and but for those footings, they would collapse and crumble away. So is it with the works of God in nature and in grace; we see the upper stages, we do not see that underneath from which they spring and on which they rest. I have sought to indicate, by way of suggestion, the direction in which we must look for the footings of the Sacramental System; and this, in order to lift the subject at once from the place of expediencies, conveniences, and utilitarian considerations, and to place it where it belongs, among things supernatural. Having done so, the way is open for a passage to the simpler and more intelligible aspects of our subject. As a practical arrangement it has other claims on confidence. Questions about fitness, adaptation, congruity, correspondence to our state and constitution, have their importance and interest; but however the system may be commended on these accounts, it must be remembered that they are not of the foundation, and that to study them belongs to a secondary department in theology For this reason it seemed necessary, before speaking particularly of such rites as Holy Baptism and Holy Communion, of Confirmation, of Holy Matrimony, of Holy Order, of Absolution, and Unction, to waive for the time the question of the intent, the value, and the effect of each, and to try and find the mysterious and recondite cause which makes them what they are, and connects them with worlds above and worlds below. There, in fact, must the line be drawn — if we are to think and speak as reverent students of Catholic theology — between the conception of sacraments as mere signs and forms, of value in the using, but devoid of intrinsic virtue, and sacraments regarded as powers of the world to come, and holding within them something of that mystery which surrounds man on every hand. And it is the more important to begin at that starting-point, because of the intense aversion of the popular mind to the thing which makes the Sacramental System a reality and a truth. For we may at once admit, and frankly, that to the conception of the system as it has been presented to you, the spirit of the age is decidedly and strongly averse. Men will take anything from us so long as we make no draft on their faith, but as soon as it comes to marvels and miracles, and results transcending the natural powers of the understanding, there is an end of their respect for our intelligence or their confidence in us as guides. There would be no objection to sacraments considered as outward forms, pictorial representations, or symbolic acts; just as there is no objection to a creed if every man is permitted to put on it what sense he pleases, or to ritual so long as it means nothing; but when we speak of sacraments as channels of grace, and supernatural agencies in the process of man's salvation, good-by at once to trust, to respect, and even to the use of polite language. Sacraments, if that is what they mean, are mummery and magic; soul-destroying, Christ-concealing inventions; a snare, a delusion, an offence to the simple, and the teachers of sacramental religion are mediæval formalists, deceived and being deceived. Baptism, for example, is well enough as a ceremony of initiation, or a sign of profession and mark of difference; nay, as such, and as performed in a particular manner, it is the badge of a sect numbering in these United States some three millions of adherents; but it cannot be an instrument of regeneration, seeing that—as the objector states it—regeneration may take place before or after the reception of baptism, but cannot by any possibility occur at the moment of the administration; while in the case of the Lord's Supper the only thing to be strenuously asserted is that "this is *not* His Body," and that "this is *not* His Blood."

An opposition so widespread and so inveterate cannot be successfully dealt with as a mere prejudice, which in time may pass away; it is the result of fundamental error on the subject of the sacraments. In such cases nothing comes of playing about the edges of the question; we must go to the root of the matter. The intense hostility to sacramental doctrine which characterizes the

Protestant mind appears to be the result of long and persistent inculcation of the principles of philosophic idealism and exaggerated spiritualism, by teachers misinformed on the origin, constitution, and destiny of man, and his relations to the universe; and until people are set right on those points they cannot see, and ought not to be expected to see, what the doctrine of the Church means and how vitally it touches us. Wherever the constitution of man, his place in the material universe, and his future destiny, bodily and spiritually, are not rightly understood; wherever he is regarded as an intelligence temporarily served by a material organism which is an encumbrance, and of which it were advantageous to be rid forever; wherever the permanence of the body in spiritual and glorified conditions is denied; where God is regarded as cutting Himself off from the universe and looking on, indifferent and isolated, while things grind along machine-like, without oversight or interference on His part; where it is forgotten that God is still a creator, and ever working as such within the world, in operations personally directed by Himself; wherever mind is exalted above heart, and man is lauded as all but a deity, and regarded as sufficient to himself without the need of outside aid, wherever it is taught that purity in religion depends on detaching one's self from the visible and palpable, and trusting to inner light, intuitions, rational processes, and subjective impressions—there, of course, man must reject the Catholic teaching on the sacraments, for it flatly contradicts every one of those cherished ideas of the natural heart. It needs no other schooling than that received from this ideal philosophy to lead a man to reject the visible and institutional in religion; to affect severe simplicity in worship; to make him suspicious of form, symbolism, and whatever addresses the senses and the imagination; to look askance and with unfriendly eye on liturgical order, exterior magnificence in worship, the visible beauty of color, ceremonial, sight, and sound, as belonging to a rudimental and unspiritual religion, and deserving no consideration from one who, as he boasts, has outgrown babyhood and come to the full stature of the intelligent and rational man. That these and the like are the serious convictions of the impugners of the teaching of the Church on the sacraments of the Gospel cannot be doubted, when we consider with what supercilious confidence they conduct themselves towards us, and how high an estimate they set on their alleged emancipation from superstition. It is a race which worldly philosophy has engendered in its womb, and nurtures at its cold, unsympathetic breast.

What can be done for men thus wandering afar from the things belonging to their peace, under the control of prejudices such as have been described, it is hard to say: but as the trouble lies at the base of all their thoughts, it seemed necessary, in treating of the sacraments of the Gospel, to begin at the beginning. For that reason I spoke to you of nature, as the handiwork of God; of creation, as originally very good; of the place of man in nature, and his intimate relations to "the creature," as St. Paul, in our version, calls it; of the development and future of man and nature, on lines trending in the same direction; of the summing up of all things in the Incarnate Word, who is called "*the first-born of every creature.*" * And having thus reminded you that "all things are ours, and that we are Christ's, and that Christ is God's," † it was suggested as natural and reasonable to suppose that indications of the relationship between man and nature may be traceable; that practical purposes may be served, by the ministration of nat-

---

* Col. 1 15. † 1 Cor iii 23

ural elements to man in his supernatural life, that through objects sanctified to a higher use, strength and grace may flow from Christ to men; that simple, natural elements may be transmuted for a strange and mystical ministry to us both in body and soul; that such transformation and exaltation of the creature carries in it the prophecy of even greater things than these; that as man, complete in a recovered body and a ransomed soul, is destined to live on in a higher state than this, so the whole creation, guided by a divine instinct, is looking out anxiously and hopefully for some benediction and help as coincident with "the redemption of our body," * that great event towards which all moves and on which all converges. Godet, in his "Studies on the Old Testament," has well and eloquently traced a progress and development through creation, which surely has not yet reached its final mark.

"On the theatre of nature unconscious life has been exercised, a slave to the senses On the stage of history the human soul has displayed the riches of life, self-conscious and free In the Church (understanding this word in its most spiritual sense) there grew up, and has since developed itself,

---

* Rom. viii. 23.

a new thing—the life of holy love, realized in Jesus Christ, and by Him communicated to us. Finally, in that supreme abode which we call heaven, this perfect life, divine in its essence, human in its form, will expand and radiate through matter then glorified." *

Thus does the material world minister to its terrestrial head, thus do material elements receive a present glorification and change for transcendental use, thus does man draw along with him the whole order in which he has his place, while advancing towards completed redemption; and here we find the meaning of a divine arrangement which extends the Incarnation through the ages, and links us to Christ, and, in Christ, to God. Such are the more recondite aspects in which this teaching challenges our faith and cheers us in the darkness of our present life.

But now, having completed the first part of our work, we may proceed to study more closely that which rises on this foundation. The bases are, indeed, mysterious, obscure, and hidden from the sight; but it is easy to study the superstructure, and note the general arrangement of the edifice, its adaptation to its purposes, and its perfect cor-

---

* "Studies on the Old Testament," p. 63

respondence with the order of the visible world and the plan according to which we and all things about us live and move and act. The region thus far traversed may be, and doubtless will be, regarded by many as a place of speculation and dreamery. Studies such as these do not commend themselves to every mind; and if, in saying what has been said, we had spoken our last word on the subject, it would have been said to no purpose in the ears of the children of this generation. But there is much more to come. Catholic theology is broad and deep; it fails us not, wherever we need its help. Profound though it be, it is no less practical. It has its commonplace side, on which it meets the commonplace mind, and challenges the attention of that class, who, disliking abstract study, want to know precisely what a thing is worth, and are not interested until it is presented in a business shape, under conditions in which they can set to with square, line, and scales, with tables of figures and a schedule of prices, and bring it down to a calculation and a commercial result. Even so the Sacramental System may challenge study and will reward it; for we hold that it is in no sense a theory, a speculation, or an invention of romantic enthusiasts, but a very plain, simple, and practical thing, by the help of which a man may live to the glory of God and the good of his fellows, if he knows the obligations which it imposes and fulfils the duties which it enjoins. Let us then proceed to consider it under some lower points of view.

To one brought up in the Anglican Church, the first thing thought of when a sacrament is mentioned is this, that it is a Sign.

> "What meanest thou by this word sacrament?"
> "I mean an outward and visible sign of an inward and spiritual grace"
> "How many parts are there in a sacrament?"
> "Two, the outward visible sign, and the inward and spiritual grace"

Here we strike a line on which the aptness of these ordinances to the wants of man comes into view. For the use of signs is so extensive that there is no part of the visible creation with which we are acquainted in which they are not employed; they are the familiar and necessary conditions to individual intercourse and combination for social action. The sign system is as high as heaven, as far spread as to the ends of the earth; all-pervading, and everywhere in use for the purposes of personal and social life.

What is a sign? Something which stands for something else; something or other, exterior, visible, palpable, audible, which signifies, and usually or always conceals, something invisible, intangible, interior. This is the meaning of the word, and if sacraments are signs, then by a sacramental system is meant a system of such signs. Now we assert, and challenge a denial of the assertion, that such a system surrounds and hems in the entire life of man. Look on the universe of which we form a part. We are on the old ground again, but now we are studying the subject from a different point of view, not meditating of matters occult and hidden in the secret working of the Almighty Creator, but taking note of the common facts of daily life; it is not now the deep mystery of nature which calls our attention, but the peculiar mode on which it has been organized and in which things present themselves for inspection.

I. God's works in nature constitute a series of products of creative power, throughout which may be discerned the two parts of the sacrament, a visible form and an invisible life. It is a universe of signs and sacraments; nature, throughout, is sacramental. The things about us, amidst which we live, move, and have our being, are subject to observation by the senses; we can explore, investigate, experiment, but full early a point is reached at which further investigation would prove useless. Elementary substances, limited and few in number, take innumerable forms. But each of these forms is a mere exterior wrapper; each veils what we call life, and what life is no man can tell.

"Life ! Who understands it ? Who has seen it ? It is like the goddess Isis, whose veil may never be lifted by mortal hand We take life as a fact, we ascertain its beginning, development, end, but we cannot explain it"

So writes a serious author. But is he right in asserting that we ascertain its beginning? Not so, except that it begins with God, and that God is life eternal. We know very little about life. One thing we know; it is impossible to point to any satisfactory experimental proof that life can be developed save from demonstrable antecedent life; that the conditions under which matter assumes the properties we call *vital* have never yet been artificially brought together.* It is a settled conviction that life in its essence is something beyond any

---

* "Winds of Doctrine being an examination of the modern theories of Automatism and Evolution" By Charles Elam, M D, pp. 78, 79, 94, 109

THE SACRAMENTAL SYSTEM APPLIED. 57

combination of physical forces; in short, that life has no physical correlate. In vain have philosophers of a certain school endeavored to establish the proposition that the earliest organisms were the natural product of the interactions of ordinary inorganic matter and force. Neither observation, experiment, nor reason gives any testimony in favor of such a view; on the contrary, the conclusion is an irresistible one, that life is in all cases due either to antecedent life or to a power and force from without that is not identical nor correlated with the ordinary physical forces.

"Supposing," says Canon Mason, "that the whole fabric of inorganic matter, with its wonders of light and heat and electricity, with its planetary systems, with the beauties of water, air, and earth, were the result of an accidental play of atoms, yet life, so far as we can see, cannot be accounted for in the same way It is as nearly certain as anything can be that the conditions of matter were at one time such—the solar system consisting of matter at a white heat—that no kind of organic life such as we are acquainted with was possible in it Organic life, then, has had a beginning in the world even if matter and force have not. How did it begin ? Experimental evidence cannot establish a negative, but the researches of men unprejudiced and competent confirm us in supposing that there is no such thing as spontaneous generation Science knows of no life which had not a living parent, and science teaches that once there were no living parents on earth to produce a life Yet here life is The chasm between the noblest form of inorganic being and the lowest form of organic—a crystal, for instance, and a cell of protoplasm—is so great that no connecting link can be found So far as we see, no evolution works gradually up to life It is a sudden, startling phenomenon, which uses matter and force for its own purposes, but which is not derived from them Whence was the first life introduced into a world which had once been incapable of harboring it, and which seems forever incapable of producing it?"*

Beneath the form, then, is an inner, unseen principle which evades search and defies comprehension. It comes downward into these forms; it is never spontaneously generated , that only which has life can give life. What it is, no one can tell us The outspread heavens, the myriad orbs of night, the solar system, earth, dry land, seas, valley and hill, the mineral, floral, and animal kingdoms all keep the secret close. What and whence is life? Matter has form, shape, and extension; it is subject to quantitative and qualitative analysis, but it is "informed," indwelt, by something else invisible, immaterial, inexplicable, which no one can describe or explain. What is life? No one knows.

---

* "Faith of the Gospel," pp 8, 9

Whence is life? Let us hear the conclusion of a great student of nature. Charles Darwin says: "I infer from analogy that probably all the organic beings which have ever lived on this earth have descended from some one form into which life was first breathed by the Creator." If that inference as to the origin of life be just, we have all that we need for the point in hand. Creation is one vast Sacramental System; an endless and overwhelming variety of outward and visible forms or signs, quickened by an invisible and incomprehensible vital force. Life is in everything; in everything it is concealed, it comes not from any natural source; it is a gift of the Creator who alone hath life in Himself. What we hold to be true of the sacraments of the Gospel is, in fact, no more than what we trace everywhere throughout creation; and to object to our claim and declaration that, although visible and material in form, they contain and convey an inward and spiritual grace and power, is as unreasonable as to deny what we certainly know to be true of everything about us which hath the breath of life; of the creatures which have a material organism, and within it a quickening principle originally derived from some region outside the bounds of the natural universe.

II. A striking illustration of this universal arrangement of God's universe is seen in man. He is, emphatically, a sacrament, and a sacrament of a very wonderful order. He has a material body, an animal soul, an immaterial and immortal spirit.* His body is the sign; made of the same elements which, otherwise combined, form the brute, the plant, the rock; within this frame is a principle of animal life, which gives him his place with the other orders of created beings; there also reside the principle of intelligence, which lifts him to a higher plane, and the spark of divine fire which carries him almost up to the place of the angels, and makes him an heir of immortal life. What then is this creature but a sacrament? What is his existence but a sacramental existence? Eye, tongue, hand, look, speech, are agents apt to reveal what is going on within. Who has ever seen a man? What we come in contact with is an outward and visible sign, eye answers to eye, hand clasps hand, voices ask and answer questions: but where or what is the real, the invisible, being, who thinks and speaks and is and lives?

III. In a universe sacramental throughout stands

---

* 1 Thess v. 23

man, himself, also, a sacrament. He lives, moreover, a sacramental life; his existence is prolonged and continued in a manner suited to his state. The elements supply what is necessary to that visible frame which contains the immaterial soul and the immortal spirit; he cannot do without their help. His daily food is a sacrament; it is not meat and drink, in their accidents, which support our life, but some principle, which, disengaged by the digestive process, goes to make up the waste of muscular tissue and nerve force, maintains the vital heat, insures the circulation of the blood, and, for a time, wards off death. Even the daily meal is, in its lower way, sacramental; man doth not live by bread alone; but God, through the use of the bread, keeps man alive and well. And so of all the actions of men; the same principle holds good, whatever we think or do or say. Speech is a sacrament of thought; an audible sign to the hearer, conveying what is in the mind. The eye has power to express or interpret hope, fear, passion, love. Books and letters are sacraments; the alphabet is a sign, conveying meaning to the reader, business transactions would be impossible without commercial and negotiable paper; fleets and armies move on signals from the chief. Man thus leads a sacramental life. It is thus with him also on the religious side; signs and forms are needed there, as everywhere else, he cannot state his faith without words, terms, and phrases proper to that use, by visible acts he holds communion with the powers above him; prayer and praise, the attitude of supplication, the sign of the cross, are appropriate to his condition; his soul is fed through agencies adapted to his state. To say that these things are unnecessary and out of place; that the use of signs and sacraments, elsewhere universal, must cease when it comes to our religious life, is to contradict common experience, and to make confusion where everything else is plain and clear.

IV. For it is not only a flat denial of the faith of the Church, but also a contradiction of our common sense to tell us that we, on our Godward side, are left, and ought to be left, without sign, symbol, visible agency, or sensible means of communication with God and access to Him. God is a spirit, without body, parts, or passions. But it is not thus that man knows Him, nor could He ever have been known to us as we need to know Him, had He remained apart from us in that eternal and incomprehensible state. The highest illustration of the Sacramental System is presented in the story of redemption.

THE SACRAMENTAL SYSTEM APPLIED 63

God, to save man, descends from heaven; He humbles Himself to our plane; He adapts Himself to that constitution which He has given us; He also is become as one of us, and wills to lead the sacramental life. Man is immortal; in knowledge of God standeth that immortality; that knowledge is brought to him through the material and the visible. Some knowledge of God may be had by study of nature, which is a visible sign, a system of signs, disclosing the eternal power and godhead. But to the end that the knowledge might be clear and full, a more intelligible revelation was employed. That revelation came on the same lines on which other knowledge comes, in a mode according with the analogies of the universe, our own constitution, and our relations toward everything that surrounds us. A sacrament is, first of all, a visible sign. Did God need such signs to make Himself known to man? Why need he use them? He is a spirit,* and "there is a spirit in man."† Might He not—to please the idealists and transcendentalists—have limited Himself to spiritual communications, made directly, without sign or medium of any sort, and so disclosed to us

---

* St. John, iv. 24. † Job, xxxii 8

whatever He pleased? It is not a question what the Almighty could or could not have done, but of what He did. He has not communicated with us in that abstract way. To have done so would have been a violation of the order of the universe, an inexplicable and embarrassing anomaly. He used the sign method and the sign language. He became a Sign and a Sacrament Himself. "The Word was made flesh, and dwelt among us"* "God sent his own Son in the likeness of sinful flesh."† "God sent forth his Son, made of a woman, made under the law." ‡ He came in such wise that men could see Him with the bodily eye, and touch and handle Him. "That which was from the beginning," saith St. John, "we have heard, we have seen with our eyes, we have looked upon, and our hands have handled."§ In the mystery of His holy Incarnation God set His seal, once more and finally, to the sacramental principle, and gave it universal application and everlasting permanence. God in Christ was and is the sacrament of sacraments. In Him are the outward and visible sign and the inward part or thing signified. The sign is a humanity, constituted complete in body, flesh,

---

* St John i. 14.   † Rom viii 3.
‡ Gal. iv. 4.   § 1 St John, i 1

THE SACRAMENTAL SYSTEM APPLIED 65

bones, spirit, and soul, like ours. The inward part or thing signified is the divine nature, united to the human in the person of the Son of God. Here are the *sacramentum* and the *res* And the inward and spiritual grace is that power which, through the Holy Ghost, flows out by many a visible sign and sacrament, from Him to us Virtue goes forth now, as it did when the blind saw at His touch, and the lame walked, and the lepers were cleansed at His spoken word. He, as "the image of the invisible God," the first-born of the whole creation,* is the most perfect instance of a sacrament that the imagination can conceive ; and in condescending to take that position in His universe He tells us, distinctly, the truth, that the principle is a universal one, and runs up and down and everywhere, throughout the entire compass of the world. †

The argument from analogy and experience, to which your attention has now been called, may be supplemented by another, from correspondence and congruity. Man, as we know, has a dual nature ; it is therefore meet and fitting that the means of his enlightenment and elevation should be adapted to

---

* Col 1 15
† See "Pearson on the Creed,' Art. II , cited by Bishop Wordsworth on Col 1 15

his twofold condition. There is a singular propriety and fitness in the Sacramental System, when we consider to whom it is applied, indeed, it is not readily conceivable how man, being in the body, could have been reached excepting through the body; nor would a religion which declined to take note of the body and made no provision for its demands deserve consideration, as a religion fit for us in our present state. I shall not dwell on this view of the subject. Some have trusted to it, as the strongest thing that could be said for our case. In fact, it is the least important in the order of arguments. It has its place, but that place is not the first, but the last. And the same remark may be made of certain philological considerations, apparently used in recommendation of the system, but really tending to restrict it. True it is that sacraments are signs, not only to the worthy receiver, but also to the outside world; as true that they have their use as seals and pledges; but these matters, compared with others, are of secondary importance. Such conceptions of the use and value of sacraments are derived from the old classical meaning of the word. The "*sacramentum*" was, as you know, the soldier's oath of allegiance and loyalty, a formula of great importance in the military ser-

THE SACRAMENTAL SYSTEM APPLIED 67

vice, announcing the intention and resolve to be true to the standard and obedient to command, and to do, in general, a soldier's duty. Such use is also in sacraments, regarded simply from the human side. In their administration and reception we note the ideas of promise, pledge, and vow, made by or for us, confirmed and ratified, and periodically reaffirmed. In them we find also, considering the publicity of their administration, a value as signs to bystanders, intimating purpose, announcing intention, inviting sympathy, and suggesting imitation. But these uses of sacraments are the lowest and last of all; important in their own place, they yield the precedence to higher considerations of the wonder-working power of God, we think first; later, of the dispositions and concurrence of man.

The first division of my work is completed. Going back to the origin of things, we have sought a foundation for the Sacramental System in the eternal counsels and plans of the Almighty, in the relation of the creature to the Creator, through the foreseen Incarnation of the eternal Son of God. We have found the system to be in accord with the constitution of the visible universe, and the nature of mankind; we have discovered its most beautiful illustration in the union of the lower and the higher natures in Jesus Christ. It is in complete accord with us, in our present state; it is necessarily and inevitably in accord with us; so that a religion which was not sacramental could not have met the wants of mankind. We find it, moreover, to be of practical value, in identifying our place among our fellow-beings, as confessors of one holy faith, and in stamping us with a peculiar impress, known and read of all men. We realize the fact that it establishes and maintains a connection between us and the supernatural order; as giving us grace, and assuring us that it has been conferred; as moving us, under a sense of awful obligation, to the consecration of heart, mind, and will to the service of God. It exercises a strong influence so long as conscience lives and acts, constraining us to the punctual discharge of assumed obligations, and maintaining that sense of dependence on the higher powers which is the characteristic of the Catholic mind. The whole field of human need and human experience seems to be covered, where the system holds sway. The believer, in his reverent acceptance of sacramental gifts from God, is, though he never may have realized it, in touch with powers and forces which broaden outward and upward, till the universe is

THE SACRAMENTAL SYSTEM APPLIED 69

swept by them; and this fleeting hour, with its issues of life and death to the souls of men, is, in sequence, one with the beginning wherein all things were made. No doubt there are forces at work among us with which we are not yet acquainted. It has been surmised, by some reverent, though perhaps enthusiastic souls, that the time may come when we shall discover a particular force, long active in the world, which has been applied to the bodies and souls of the redeemed in Christ, through the sacraments of the Church, precisely as other forces, well known to us to-day, are working in the physical order.

Such is the Sacramental System, in the broadest light under which it can be presented to the mind. It were vain to hope, at this day, for a general acceptance of the facts concerning this grace of God; "the natural man receiveth not the things of the Spirit of God, for they are foolishness unto him: neither can he know them, because they are spiritually discerned"* The name of sacraments may be retained, and their use may continue, where the life has gone out of them; and the life does so go out, as soon as the outward and inward are divided,

---

* 1 Cor. ii. 14.

for then the outward remains a dead and lifeless sign, while the inward evaporates into a volatile vapor of sentiment. The principle of rationalism, applied to these mystical and beneficent rites, leaves them to us as mere memorials, emblems of absent things, or occasions on which we are to perform something for our own advantage, instead of receiving the "unspeakable gift" of God. In the narrowness of sectarian religious temper and the poverty and timidity of modern thought, men have lost hold of what they ought to have held fast forever. Some reject the sacraments altogether; some retain them under a protest that they mean nothing and confer nothing; in submitting to baptism or receiving the Lord's Supper they have no thought beyond doing something for their neighbors to look at, or signifying the vitality of what they style their faith, or announcing their personal religious convictions, or stirring up a tender recollection. The supernatural element dies out of these degraded rites; "ordinances" only are left, which neither convey grace nor link man and God together; which are commended solely on grounds of convenience or expediency; which serve a utilitarian purpose as badges of respectability, but in themselves are nothing. It is a striking feature of the times in which we live, that the broadest and deepest views in theology are popularly considered to be narrow, while the narrowest are denominated broad. So, in the days of Isaiah, men called evil good and good evil; they put darkness for light and light for darkness, bitter for sweet and sweet for bitter.* The men who hold the most advanced sacramental doctrine are reviled as narrow and exclusive. It does not occur to any to ask what these so-called narrow men believe, how far the application of their faith extends, or how exceedingly narrow in contrast are the ideas of their opponents. For, really, the man who denies the Sacramental System, who says of baptism that it is a mere outward washing, or a rite of initiation, and confers no inward and spiritual grace, and that the Lord's Supper, if it were intended to continue in use, is, after all, no more than a memorial meal, and has no power but that of affecting our feelings and deepening our sympathies with Him who so ate before He died; this man is not really broad at all, but the narrowest of the narrow, though he should call all the world to come and sit down to meat with him, and accept everybody to his fellowship without

---

* Isa. v. 20

regard to initiatory lavation or particular statement of faith. On the other hand, that man who intelligently holds the belief of the Church and the fathers on these great themes is the real broad churchman, though he maintain, as he ought to, that mysteries so sacred as these should not be open to any rash foot, but must be defended from profanation and reserved for those who have the signed and certified pass and order to admit them to the presence of the King.

A few words in conclusion of this branch of my subject. The destruction of the Sacramental System, as a wonder-working power of the world to come, is at once effected by separating the sign from the thing signified and leaving a bare sign and nothing more. Happily we, as a Church, are protected from that error by the clearest declarations in our standards.

" Sacraments ordained of Christ," says Article XXV., " be not only badges or tokens of Christian men's profession, but rather they be certain sure witnesses and effectual signs of grace and God's good will towards us, by the which He doth work invisibly in us, and doth not only quicken but strengthen and confirm our faith in Him "

And so of Holy Baptism, it is declared in Article XXVII. to be "not only a sign of profession and mark of difference, whereby Christian men are discerned from others that be not christened, but it is also a sign of regeneration or new birth, whereby, as by an instrument, they that receive baptism rightly are grafted into the Church."

And elsewhere we read:

"Thus much we must be sure to hold, that in the Supper of the Lord there is no vain ceremony, no bare sign, no untrue figure of a thing absent. *But,* as the Scripture saith, *the table of the Lord, the bread and cup of the Lord, the memory of Christ, the annunciation of His death, yea, the communion of the Body and Blood of the Lord, in a marvellous incorporation, which by the operation of the Holy Ghost (the very bond of our conjunction with Christ) is through faith wrought in the souls of the faithful, whereby not only their souls live to eternal life, but they surely trust to win to their bodies a resurrection to immortality.*"*

The Zwinglian theory, that sacraments are nothing but memorials of Christ, and badges of a Christian profession, is that one which can by no possible jugglery with the English tongue be reconciled with the formularies of our Church; the principle is contradicted by the entire cast of our sacramental offices, and by every word in them which can convey an idea of their meaning. It is well for

---

* "An Homily of the Worthy Receiving and Reverent Esteeming of the Sacrament of the Body and Blood of Christ." Part I.

us that this is the case; for the Zwinglian theory is simply rationalism in a religious dress; and it should be held as a matter of obligation and a point of honor to maintain that we, as a Church, have neither art nor part therein. Nor need it cause anxiety, however painful the discovery, to find men among us infected with the views of the Swiss reformer, and even carried so far by admiration for him as to make their compliments to him as "the clear-headed and intrepid Zwingle." After all, such persons deceive no one but themselves, not only within the Church, but outside it also, her position is understood; and I take occasion to acknowledge our obligation to a learned and eminent Presbyterian divine, lately deceased, the Rev. Henry I. Van Dyke, for the good service rendered us in his free dissection of a much-admired dignitary of the Anglican Church, Dean Stanley, whose views about the Holy Communion he describes as "the ripest and bitterest fruit of rationalizing about the Lord's Supper."* It is perfectly true, as Dr. Van Dyke

---

* "The Church, her Ministry and Sacraments." The Stone Lectures at Princeton, 1890, by Henry I Van Dyke, D D, Pastor of the Second Presbyterian Church of Brooklyn (A D F Randolph, New York), pp 175, 176. The whole passage here referred to will be found in the Appended Notes, No II

goes on to say, that the sign theory of the sacraments is "the symbol of rationalism in its bald and naked shape." That theory, however strongly it may commend itself to individuals here and there, is foreign to the standards of the Church. It flourishes as faith in the supernatural grows weak; it dies when that faith revives. The voice of Catholic Christendom, as duly and clearly heard in our Offices and Articles, reproves and rebukes it; and of late, our hold on the higher truth and the deeper mysteries has strengthened, under observation of the result of giving away the treasure committed to our keeping. The words of Bishop Harold Browne may be adopted as expressive of the judgment and belief of the Church from which we have our Orders, that "the sacraments of the Gospel not only promise Christ, but to those who receive them in faith they are means whereby God gives Christ to the soul." *

---

* " Exposition of the Thirty-nine Articles," Vol II p 382

III.

THE LESSER SACRAMENTS.

LECTURE III.

THE LESSER SACRAMENTS.

IT may be said, by way of general remark upon the Sacramental System, that, with a widening appreciation of the nature of that system and its application to us in our life, there will come a disinclination to restrict the number of these means of grace. On that point differences are found throughout the Church. The Latins fix the number of the sacraments to seven; the Eastern churches follow them in that particular The number was not defined in the Confession of Augsburg, but it enumerates three as "having the command of God and the promise of the grace of the New Testament." Luther admitted three—Baptism, the Lord's Supper, Penitence. Cranmer, in his Catechism, says:

"Our Lorde Jesus Christ hath instituted and annexed to the gospel thre sacraments or holy seales, of his covenant and lege made with us And by these thre, God's ministers do worke with us in the name and place of God (yea, God himselfe worketh with us) to confirme us in our faith, and to asserten us that we are the lyvely membres of God's trew churche and the chosen people of God, to whome the gospell is sent, and that all those things belong to us wherof the promises of the gospel make mention. The first of these sacramentes is baptisme, by the which we be borne again to a new and heavenly lyfe, and be receaued into God's churche and congregation which is the foundation and piller of the treuth. The seconde is absolution or the authoritie of the Kayes, whereby we be absolued from such synnes as we be fallen into after our baptisme. The thirde sacramente is the communion or the Lordes Supper, by the whiche we be fedde and nourished and fortified in the faith of the ghospell and knowlege of Christ, that by this fode we maye growe more and more in newnes of lyfe, so that we maye be no longer children, but maye waxe perfecte men, and ful growen in Christ."

The mind of the Anglican Church on this point is to be gathered from Article XXV, the Catechism, and the Book of Homilies. In a guarded manner, and with some explanatory comment, she limits the number of the sacraments to two. She does not say that there are two sacraments *and no more*, but that there are two only which are, to mankind in general, necessary to salvation.

Precise statements such as these, with limitation of the number of God's sacraments, are obviously the result of constraining causes; and chiefly due to the tendency to systematize in theology, and to a reaction against false or exaggerated teaching. As the Church was compelled, by the inroads of heresy, to mark with greater exactness of definition the lines of the Christian faith, so in the matter of the sacraments she has been forced by circumstances to make artificial limitations, and to narrow the field of view. What breadth, what grandeur, in the first conception of the Sacramental System! Christ a sacrament, man a sacrament, leading, in body and soul, a sacramental life; the earth, in its several kingdoms, and the vast outlying universe, all having their sacramental cast and character; religion sacramental throughout; sacraments everywhere, and hardly anything which is not sacramental! Thus do the old fathers and doctors of the Church appear to have regarded the subject, in the freshness and enthusiasm of early days, ere yet exigencies had arisen which called for definitions and restrictions. Anything in or under which divine power was veiled, was, in their eyes, a sacrament; even the implements used in working great wonders were styled by that name. Speaking of this wide application of the term, Jeremy Taylor says:

"When God appointed the bow in the clouds to be a sacrament and the memorial of a promise, he made it our comfort, but his own sign 'I will remember my covenant between me and the earth, and the waters shall no more be a flood to destroy all flesh.' When Elisha threw the wood into the waters of Jordan—'sacramentum ligni, the sacrament of the wood,' Tertullian calls it—that chip made the iron swim, not by any natural or infused power, but that was the sacrament or sign at which the divine power then passed on to effect an emanation. When Elisha talked with the King of Israel about the war with Syria, he commanded him to smite upon the ground, and he smote thrice and stayed. This was 'sacramentum victoriæ,' the sacrament of his future victory. The sacraments are God's signs, the opportunities of grace and action." *

To return to a consideration of the mind of our Church as to the number of the sacraments. On that point her teaching is wise and clear. Making it a condition that a sacrament, to take the highest grade, should have been "ordained by Christ Himself," she finds two only of that class, Baptism and the Supper of the Lord.† These tower preeminently above all other rites to which the name of sacrament has been or may be applied; these, and these only, were instituted by our blessed Lord Himself with reference to the wants of mankind in general, without distinction of sex, race, circum-

---

* "Worthy Communicant," ch. 1 sect. III.
† See "Bishop Forbes on the Thirty-nine Articles," Vol II. p 445.

stance, or vocation. But she does not deny that in addition to these there are sacraments of an inferior grade. The sacrament of Matrimony is mentioned by that name in one of the Homilies, as "that which knitteth man and wife in perpetual love;" while of Absolution and others it is acknowledged that they are also sacraments, in some sense.

"Absolution is no such sacrament as Baptism and the Communion are . . . it lacks the promise of remission of sin, as all other sacraments besides the two above-named do . . . they are not sacraments, in the same signification that the two forenamed sacraments are." "Although there are retained, by the order of the Church of England, besides these two, certain other rites and ceremonies about the institution of ministers in the Church, matrimony, confirmation of children, and the visitation of the sick, yet no man ought to take these for sacraments, in such signification and meaning as the sacrament of Baptism and the Lord's Supper are."

This language clearly indicates the position of the Anglican communion on the subject. There are two great sacraments of the Gospel, ordained by the Lord Himself, and generally necessary to salvation. But, in a general acceptation, the name of a sacrament may be attributed to anything whereby an holy thing is signified; and therefore it is correctly applied to those other rites "commonly called sacraments, so far as they are ministered in true Gospel wise, and do not imply a corrupt following of the apostles." "They have not like nature of sacraments with Baptism and the Lord's Supper," says the Article; but that they have no sacramental nature or character whatever is not affirmed in our standards. In fact, there is good reason for insisting on the sacramental character and quality of the ordinances now referred to, and their affinity to the great "sacraments of the Gospel;" for they aid to keep before us, with reference to some of the most important actions of life, and particularly with reference to the sacred ministry, the alliance between the natural and supernatural, and to stamp a special seal of holiness and religious obligation on our relations to the Church and to each other. To deny the sacramental quality in these ordinances is to do what can be done to take God out of them, and relegate them to the line of secular transactions; to affirm that quality in them is to declare our adhesion to a Supernatural Religion.

Take Confirmation, for instance. It cannot be considered as barred out by the language of Article XXV. It is retained among us on the very ground that it is "a following of the apostles;" surely not a "corrupt" one. Deny to it the sacramental character, and what is left? A ceremony in which the person confirmed is the principal, if not the only personal, actor. He comes to confirmation merely in order to assume obligations previously incurred by others in his name; it is now his business to justify the act of his friends and relieve them of a responsibility; he comes forward under a sense of duty to take his place in the Church and make his oath as a soldier of Christ. This is all true as far as it goes, but to stop with this is to keep on our side of the line and decline to cross it and get on God's side. There is no mystery in such steps as these; no trace of supernatural workings; the action, so far, is simply that of the man admitting a duty and discharging an obligation. A rite so commonplace as this would afford nothing for theological analysis, and the failure to perceive the sacramental quality in Confirmation is the necessary consequence of exclusive attention to the part performed by the candidate. A higher field is entered the instant we turn our eyes above. God the Holy Ghost: the moment He appears, the scene and the conception change, and we feel the throbbing of the sacramental force. It is He that confirms; by Him the sevenfold gifts are exhibited and imparted; from Him a special benediction and power descend upon the young soldier of Christ. And these constitute a gracious gift conferred by instrumental means, and in the act of the laying-on of hands by the chief pastor of the Church; so that from the sphere above, whence at first came spiritual life, we receive a renewal of the vital gift at a special point of danger. Where these things are felt and realized—and we believe that they are widely felt and realized among us, and more and more appreciated every day—the sacramental character of the ordinance can hardly be denied. Here, surely, is an outward and visible sign, most tender and impressive, in the imposition of pastoral hands on the head of the child; here also is an inward and spiritual grace, in the gifts of the Holy Ghost; and though we miss the special mark in the institution of this rite by Christ Himself, yet it comes so near it that it could hardly be nearer. This is no "corrupt following of the apostles," but a true and sincere following of them, "after whose example" the thing is done; and whatever the holy apostles did we must believe to have been done, if not on the verbal suggestion of the Master, at least under the guidance of the Holy Spirit sent to them from the Father. We do not hesitate to call Confirmation a minor sacrament, a sacrament of a lower class; not such as the higher two, but precious as a means of grace, apt to that perilous age when, as the world exhibits its first strong allurements, the child of the Church is strengthened with might by the Spirit in the inner man, confirmed in all holy desires and fortified with weapons by which to withstand the temptations of the world, the flesh, and the devil. Finally, the significance of this rite is shown in the fact that it is the door of entrance to the altar; "there shall none be admitted to the Holy Communion until such time as he be confirmed, or be ready and desirous to be confirmed." *

So with Holy Matrimony. In the case of that sacred rite we are happily able to point to the authorized use of the title; it is spoken of as "a sacrament which knitteth man and wife in perpetual love." † Holy Matrimony is "an honorable estate, instituted of God in the time of man's innocency, signifying unto us the mystical union between Christ and His Church, which holy estate Christ adorned and beautified with His presence and first miracle that He wrought in Cana of Galilee." How appropriately, how rightly, is it called among

---

* Rubric at the end of the Order of Confirmation
† Book of Homilies

us, "the Sacrament of Matrimony"! What can be gained by denying its sacramental character? How great is our advantage in being able to face the horrible spectre of divorce with a strong affirmation, supported by our formularies, that in Holy Matrimony, when rightly solemnized in the Church, God gives the man and the woman divine and supernatural grace sufficient to enable them to be faithful till parted by death! Marriage, divested of its sacramental character, becomes substantially a secular ordinance; there is no sacred mystery about it, and no grace, it might be regarded as but a business partnership, dissoluble by the contractors whenever they think it desirable to separate and form new alliances, an affair wholly within the purview of the civil magistrate, and to which the offices of the Church confer merely a religious and edifying flavor. The act of joining a man and woman together as husband and wife is essentially a civil ceremony; no special form is necessary; the union is a social compact, perpetual obligations are not incurred; for any one of a dozen causes the contract may be broken and the union dissolved. These are the results of the application of rationalistic principles to that relation on which depends the purity of society and the permanence of the state; and from such bald rationalism, under whose influence the cancer of divorce eats ever more deeply into our social system, we appeal to the principles of the Church and the sanctions of a sacramental religion. HOLY MATRIMONY is the marriage in the Church; that adjective is the characteristic note of sacramentals. It is a mystery, a sacred thing, the introduction into "a holy estate." It symbolizes the union of the Incarnate Son of God with the Church which is His Body. It makes a man and a woman one flesh by a bond which cannot be broken so long as they live. For the permanence of the union they are not to rely solely on natural powers; so unstable, so frail, so careless of duty and obligation, are the fallen beings whom God hath joined together, that supernatural grace is needed to enable them to live and love, in truth and loyalty to each other, till death. The trials and temptations which inevitably come upon the married are many and great; domestic peace is often endangered, and the union imperilled, wherefore this relation must be entered into "soberly, advisedly, discreetly, reverently and in the fear of God." And to those who thus enterprise it, there comes a special gift from above, enabling them "surely to perform and keep the vow and covenant betwixt them made." There is nothing secular and civil in these ideas; they are sacramental throughout; in this holy office there are prayers and benedictions, outward and visible signs and forms, the giving and receiving a ring, the joining hands, the words in betrothal, the solemn vow and plight of troth. Who shall say, in view of the statistics of marriage and divorce among us, that one word can be spared, that one expression is unnecessary, which helps to realize the sanctity, the divine character, the sacramental cast, of the relation between man and wife?

And so, once more, of Holy Order. The title implies the sacramental character. We speak of Holy Baptism, Holy Communion, and Holy Matrimony; so, likewise, of Holy Order. That prefix "holy" determines the place of the ordinance in the Church; it marks the distinction between a profession which any man may undertake of his own motion, or to which one can induct another at will, and a sacred office exercised among us by persons duly set apart by apostolic authority. The question of the ministry is the burning question of the hour: whether it is to be regarded as a human calling or as a divine institution; whether all ministries are equal in validity. On this point there would have been less contention among us if the sacramental idea had been more distinctly kept before the people; if they had been reminded, in language not to be misunderstood by the most obtuse, that a special grace and power accompany the laying-on of hands in Ordination. In that solemn and impressive function we find outward and visible signs, in the imposition of pastoral hands, the delivery of sacred books, the recital of words denoting the transmission of official authority; the gift of the Holy Ghost is also imparted, to make the deacon, priest, or bishop apt and meet for his vocation. The men thus set apart, according to the ancient form and rules of the historic Church, by persons who, since the apostles' time, have been thus handing down a sacred office, must be thenceforth distinguished, not only from their brethren in secular life, but also from all ministries pretending to no sacramental or superhuman character. Experience has demonstrated the importance of insisting on the true import of the Ordinal, in order to forestall the efforts strenuously made, to divest the Christian Ministry of its sacred quality, to lower the Clergy to the level of mere presidents of assemblies or mouthpieces of congregations, and to represent them as only men like other men, depending on their native powers and good intentions, but disclaiming the possession of any higher qualification for the work of ministry to their brethren.

Another means of grace demands our consideration. It is variously known as Absolution, Penitence, and Penance. The fact has been already noted that, in the Confession of Augsburg, three sacraments are enumerated, Baptism, the Lord's Supper, and Penitence. Provision of some sort, for the removal of post-baptismal sin, has always been made in the Church. The subject claims our reverent attention, and particularly at this point, because the provision referred to has always been, and must as a matter of course be, sacramental. "Almighty God," we are told, "hath given power and authority to His ministers to declare and pronounce to His people, being penitent, the absolution and remission of their sins." Whenever and wherever they exercise that power, they minister along sacramental lines; it is an office which no man under the grade of the priesthood can perform. The people may indeed confess their sins one to another, after the counsel of St. James; friend to friend, husband to wife, wife to husband, child to parent, they may speak to one another, confidently and comfortingly, of the loving kindness of the Lord; but if any desire—and no wish is more natural or more frequently expressed—a formal and official declaration that his own particular sins are forgiven, he must go to some one duly commissioned to give him satisfactory assurance on that point. He may seek it in the Church; the absolution in the Matin or Evening office, the more solemn absolution in the office of the Holy Communion, are true absolutions, applicable and effectual to any burdened soul which, by faith, appropriates the precious gift. Or else he may seek it in private, where a minute confession can be made, and the particulars of soul sickness disclosed to the physician; and, in that way, to many, the word of absolution seems to come home more closely and with a more direct and personal application. But wherever or whenever this power is exercised it appears impossible to divest it of a sacramental force, because a gracious gift is there, well won by the sacrifice to pride by which it is purchased. Nay, let us observe, moreover, how close is the connection between the earthly priest in absolution, and the Great High Priest above, and how distinctly this office bespeaks an extension of the Incarnation. Let us reverently consider the healing of the sick of the palsy, related in St. Mark, ii. 3–12. God can forgive sins. The scribes knew that, and when they heard Jesus say, with authority, "Son, thy sins be forgiven thee," they raised their protest, instantly, and cried with indignation, "Why doth this man thus speak blasphemies? Who can forgive sins but God alone?" The word of Jesus, in answer, denoted, substantially, the bringing of a new force among us. As man, did He forgive. He does not speak thus: "That ye may know that *I* have power on earth to forgive sins," as if arguing, "therefore I am God," a different point is proposed to them: "Know ye that the Son of man hath that power" True as the former conclusion is, something else is suggested here. The power to absolve is now lodged in Christ as man; to Him, as the Son of man, is extended a prerogative of God. There is a parallel passage in St. John, v. 27: "He hath authority to execute judgment also, because He is the Son of man." We all admit and feel the force of this limitation; man shall be judged by One who has man's own nature. Is it other than a prejudice which prevents us from seeing the same idea in this passage in St. Mark? Jesus, in forgiving sins, exercised the authority belonging to Him as the omnipotent and eternal Son; and yet He puts it thus to them, that what He does, He does as man. It was distinctly a part of His ministry of reconciliation; and when he committed that ministry of reconciliation to men, He gave them, ministerially, that power which, in its first exercise, awakened such indignation, caused such astonishment, and received so ample a proof of the right of the speaker to exercise it. Henceforth, the sons of men on earth have power to forgive sins, subject to the conditions imposed by the Incarnate Son of God. Belief in the remission of sins by sacramental means is an article of the Christian Faith as contained in the Nicene Creed. The power of absolution is exercised by the Holy Ghost in the sacrament of Baptism. It is exercised by the priest, when he administers to the faithful the sacrament of Holy Communion. It is exercised now publicly, and anon privately, in the absolutions declared and pronounced to the penitent. To that end some be made priests. "Receive the Holy Ghost for the office and work of a priest in the Church of God. Whose sins thou dost forgive, they are forgiven; and whose sins thou dost retain, they are retained." *

On this subject of Absolution, Penitence, or Penance, we are put on our defence, through the in-

---

* See " The Ordering of Priests "

tense and bitter prejudices and hostility awakened by the mere mention of the word. On no point are men so sensitive, on none do they become so speedily excited; auricular confession is regarded as a term taken from the vocabulary of the Evil One himself. Therefore the theologians of the Church have been at the pains to arrange and publish catenæ of authorities on this point, in defence of their position, and in deprecation of the astonishing ignorance on the subject. It is not known, or it is intentionally concealed, that the practice of private confession and the doctrine of absolution have come down to us with the recommendation of a great number of writers and teachers of unimpeachable Protestant character, and have the authority of the most highly venerated names in the Anglican Church On this point reference may be made to a pamphlet, by the Rev. C. N. Gray, entitled "A Statement on Confession," and reprinted in this city in 1872, with an introduction by one of the most learned of the professors of this Seminary, the Rev. Milo Mahan.* The student who desires to pursue the subject to a farther point should read Dr. Pusey's preface to his translation of the Abbé

---

* See Appended Notes, No III.

Gaume's "Manual for Confessors." In that exhaustive document, one hundred and seventy-four octavo pages in length, he has demonstrated the lawfulness of the practice so fully and so ably that nothing further can be added or desired. I cannot refrain from quoting the summary with which he brings the preface to a close.

"I thought it a work of charity to bring before those who would hear some portion of the evidence that the very chief of our divines have recognized confession and absolution as a provision of our Church for the healing of our infirmities and the cure of diseases which might otherwise fester and bring death upon the soul

"It may, anyhow, startle some that what they have been ignorantly declaiming against, as undermining the system of the Church of England, has been maintained by the most zealous of her defenders, that what they have condemned as Roman has been claimed by controversialists of ours against Rome, that what they have spoken against as injurious to the soul, and interfering between it and its Redeemer, has been valued by some who lived in closest union with him Some may be healthfully ashamed that they have declaimed against the practice as unprotestant, when it is advocated in all the Lutheran formulæ, some that they declaimed against it as undermining the Reformation, seeing that it was advocated by reformers such as Cranmer, Ridley, and Latimer, some, who have been pressing upon the bishops to put down it and us, may be checked in their eagerness when they see that four archbishops and twenty-one bishops, of repute as writers, have more or less strongly advocated it, that ten bishops or more, in their visitation articles, inquired whether their clergy had invited their people to confession, some of intellect may, perhaps, pause, as if they *may* have been mistaken—anyhow they cannot pooh-pooh it—when they see such names as Berkeley, Hooker, Sanderson, Barrow, Pearson, against them, some of unction may hesitate when they see such as Bishops Hall, Andrewes, Ken, J Taylor, Wilson, G Herbert, on the other side, some, who conscientiously say 'The Bible and the Bible only,' even while their tradition overrides the plain teaching of the Bible, may be startled to see 'the immortal Chillingworth'—as some used to call him—even vehemently inviting to what they themselves vehemently condemn"*

In palliation of the temper with which many estimable persons so strenuously—might I not say so viciously?—oppose the teaching of this great cloud of witnesses, it may be said that they do not appreciate the difference between the Roman and the Anglican Churches on the subject of Absolution. That difference is fundamental. In the Roman Church they have a *"Sacrament of Penance,"* necessary to salvation; it restores to the recipient the perfect purity which he is supposed to have regained

---

* Pusey's translation of Abbé Gaume's " Manual for Confessors," preface, pp 151-153.

THE LESSER SACRAMENTS 99

in baptism; it is the sole means of obtaining pardon for post-baptismal sin; it is the indispensable condition to the reception of Holy Communion. In the Anglican Church Absolution—for we have no sacrament of Penance in the Roman sense of the word—is a simple privilege of the faithful. To make confession privately to a priest is not matter of obligation; it is not a general duty; it is not enforced; it is not recommended for general use; its practice gives no right to self-laudation on the ground of a higher status in duty to the Church, nor may they who decline to do so be justly charged with shortcoming in their duty. The mind of this Church has been fully and happily expressed in the well-known passage in the 1st Book of King Edward VI.:

"And if there be any of you whose conscience is troubled and grieved in anything, lacking comfort or counsel, let him come to me, or to some other discreet and learned Priest, taught in the law of God, and confess and open his sin and grief secretly, that he may receive such ghostly counsel, advice, and comfort that his conscience may be relieved, and that of us—as of the Ministers of God and of the Church—he may receive comfort and Absolution, to the satisfaction of his mind, and avoiding of all scruple and doubtfulness, requiring such as shall be satisfied with a general Confession not to be offended with them that do use, to their further satisfying, the auricular and secret confession to the Priest, nor those also which think needful or convenient, for the quietness of their own consciences, particularly to open their sins to the Priest, to be offended with them that are satisfied with their humble confession to God, and the general Confession to the Church, but in all things to follow and keep the rule of charity, and every man to be satisfied with his own conscience, not judging other men's minds or consciences, whereas he hath no warrant of God's Word to the same."

Such is the view of Absolution held by the great divines to whom the revival of the lsat half-century was due, and such is the view of teachers nearer our own day who represent the mind of the Church. According to them, Absolution is not "a sacrament of the Gospel" necessary to acceptance with God, but a privilege of those who are drawn to seek it under the sense of sin, and a help to certain spirits who feel a special need. It is to be regretted that there is a disposition to pass beyond the Anglican line and to swing far over towards that of the Church of Rome; that we have among us enthusiastic persons who, if they do not actually insist on confession as matter of obligation, go very near to that; who subject timid and sensitive individuals to a moral suasion on that point tantamount to compulsion and command. To this tendency may be due the strong reaction against a helpful and salutary practice, of which many would have availed themselves if they had been led and not driven. If men had been content to follow strictly the line traced out for them by our great Anglican divines, and by such teachers and fathers of our own communion as Mahan and Ewer, it would have been better for us all. There is no doubt as to the sentiments of Pusey and Liddon on this point. Dr. Liddon, in a letter recently published, says:

"The question of private confession is left by our Prayer-book to the decision of the individual conscience, and it is difficult for any other person to settle, because it must be settled in view of a spiritual history known only to the soul itself and to God"

"Confession is medicine and not food, and is to be used when needed, and not as merely a matter of periodical propriety when the conscience feels that no need exists " *

---

* The letter from which these quotations are made was an answer to one who asked Dr Liddon's opinion on the subject of private confession, the writer stating that he had been taught as a youth to use confession, but that for a long time he had neglected its use, also quoting language which suggested that it was sufficient to confess our sins to our Great High Priest in heaven, without confessing them in the presence of any earthly priest as well.

"CHRIST CHURCH, OXFORD, March, 1883.
" *My Dear* ———.

"The question of private confession is left by our Prayer-book to the decision of the individual conscience and it is difficult for any other person to settle, because it must be settled in view of a spiritual history known only to the soul itself, and to God

Our own revered Mahan—"*clarum et venerabile nomen !*"—expressed himself as follows:

"I have never taught or practised any doctrine of confes-

"I have myself used confession whenever I have needed it ever since 1847, and have never regretted it I think it braces the soul as nothing else does, while the absolution that follows is a more direct and peremptory application of the absolving power left by Our Lord to His Church than the more general formulæ of the Daily and Communion Services

"I have felt too, as regards my own case, that Bishop Butler's general doctrine about the 'safer' course in questions of conduct points distinctly to the practice

"Perhaps, too, it ought to be considered that there is some risk in giving up any religious practice which has once been adopted

"In saying this, I do not forget that confession is medicine and not food, and is to be used when needed, and not as merely a matter of periodical propriety, when the conscience feels that no need exists But there is risk, when a person has once used confession, in neglecting to use it if the conscience suggests it.

"I have a true affection for ———, whose language you quote, but should doubt whether he has ever used confession in his life, and when this is the case, a man can only look at the question from one side, and make *a priori* guesses as to what may happen in a contingency of which he has no practical knowledge.

"Notwithstanding the finiteness and imperfections of the earthly minister, and the omniscience and tenderness of our Great High Priest in heaven, the former does, by Christ's commission, help us, if we will, to repent and make a great moral effort which is NOT made so easily when we are alone.

"If you rightly quote the language, it seems to suggest that the earthly priest is *in place of* the heavenly, whereas, if he does his duty, he leads us up to Him

"I am, Dear ———,
"Ever yours,
"H P LIDDON."

sion without carefully guarding against the notion of *compulsion* which is the gist of the Roman doctrine. . . . In all my innumerable answers on confession, on which I have been appealed to by all sorts of men, and for all sorts of purposes, I have invariably taught, *first of all*, that confession should always be voluntary and unforced ; I might almost say that I *hate* enforced confession, believing it to be destructive of the chief good of confession "

To the same effect are the following words of Dr. Ewer, some time rector of St. Ignatius' Church in this city:

"I hold that sins are forgiven to the faithful baptized, by God, without confession to man, and, therefore, that the sacrament of Absolution is not to be 'obtruded upon men's consciences as a matter necessary to salvation ' But I hold that such confession, previous to Absolution, although not peremptorily commanded to be used by all, nor set up as a matter necessary to salvation for any, is yet not only permitted but, under certain circumstances, advised by the Anglican Communion " *

To one other rite must reference be made.

"Extreme Unction," says Bishop Harold Browne, "is an ordinance concerning which we differ from the Church of Rome more than on the other four. We admit the proper

---

* Correspondence between the Right Reverend the Bishop of Connecticut and the Rev. F C Ewer, D D , Rector of Christ Church, New York, on the Doctrine of the Church touching the Seven Catholic Sacraments, p 15

use of Confirmation, Confession, Orders, and Matrimony; but Extreme Unction we neither esteem to be a sacrament nor an ordinance of the Church at all. As used in the modern Church of Rome, it implies unction with olive oil, blessed by the bishop, and applied by the priest to the five senses of the dying man. It is considered as conveying God's pardon and support in the last hour. It is administered when all hope of recovery is gone, and generally no food is permitted to be taken after it. The Roman Catholic controversialists," he continues, "can find no primitive authority for this ordinance. the Greeks still practice Unction, but do not consider it a sacrament."*

Unction, as thus practised in the Roman Church, is precisely what our Article describes as a "corrupt following of the apostles." But between unction *more Romanensium*, and unction as described and recommended by St. James, there is a difference. Of the latter Bishop Forbes of Brechin has spoken in words which I quote as covering the case:

"The unction of the sick is the Lost Pleiad of the Anglican firmament. One must at once confess and deplore that a distinctly Scriptural practice has ceased to be commanded in the Church of England. Excuses may be made of 'corrupt following of the apostles,' in that it was used, contrary to the mind of St. James, when all hope of restoration of bodily health was gone; but it cannot be denied that there has been

---

* "Exposition of the XXXIX Art.," Vol II pp 317-319

practically lost an apostolic practice, whereby, in case of grievous sickness, the faithful were anointed and prayed over, for the forgiveness of their sins, and to restore them, if God so willed, or to give them spiritual support in their maladies.

. The meagreness of tradition is replaced in some measure by the agreement of the Greeks, the Armenians, the Nestorians, and all the Orientals, with the Latins on this subject, so that one cannot doubt that a sacramental use of anointing the sick has been from the beginning "*

Faithful to the old customs, the Church of England appointed a service for the Unction of the Sick in her first Reformed Prayer-book. An office for the same purpose appears in the Non-Jurors' Liturgy of 1718, and also in the "Liturgy for the Church of England" compiled by William Whiston, 1713. The unction of the sick was lawful, and in occasional use in the Episcopal Church in Scotland, in 1784, when the Scottish bishops Kilgour, Skinner, and Petrie consecrated and entered into a "Concordat" with our own Seabury; the saintly and ascetic Bishop Jolly, of Moray, was wont to anoint the sick, after the example of St. James, without let, hinderance, or protest. There are not wanting, among the bishops of the American Church, some who concur in deploring the loss of

---

* "Exposition of the XXXIX. Art ," Vol II pp 463–467

this primitive ordinance, and predicting its restoration among us at some propitious time.

To sum up what has now been presented to your consideration, on the subject of several minor ordinances in the Church. While there appears to be no ground in Scripture or antiquity for limiting the sacraments to a precise number, we must regard the position of the Anglican Communion on this point to be reverent and wise. Many ordinances come forth to view, as we consider the relation of men to the Almighty Father through the medium of His Incarnate Son, and the needed application of the Gospel gifts. Let it be our aim to study these great mysteries with a ready will to take in the whole truth; and let the same mind be in us which was in the ancient fathers and doctors of the Church. A narrow rationalism should not confine us, whether it be that bred of the innate pride of the human heart, or that same temper intensified by the idea of apparent growth in knowledge of many things. Formal and restrictive statements, though appealing to the love of systematic arrangement, and conferring, as they do, no doubt, an air of rounded finish, should, on the very ground that they approach the line of the artificial, be regarded with mistrust. Nothing must be allowed to conceal or obscure the facts, that the entire system of the Gospel has a sacramental cast; that human nature was constructed on a sacramental plan; that man's life, in nature and in grace alike, is sacramental in its character; and that, if we are to accept Bible teaching simply and naturally, these conditions are never to change, but to be prolonged and continued in our eternal state. For, though the " inward part or thing signified " in our present vital union with Christ will then be realized in an all-glorious and inconceivably blessed fulness, yet we believe that it will be realized in a form; in the form of an immortal, glorious, powerful, and incorruptible life, but still a corporal life; the life of the new body of the resurrection, which, like the glorious and glorified Body of the Ascended Lord, shall live and abide forever, never to be divided from the Godhead in His Person.* All ordinances, be they greater or lesser, which help us in the establishment or maintenance of the union with Christ, have a place in the Gospel, and an honor as Sacraments or Sacramentals in His Church.

The wider the view we take of this subject, the broader its application to the relations of our life,

---

* See Article IV , " Of the Resurrection of Christ."

as members of the family and the Church, as pilgrims and strangers here, as subject to unfavorable influences from every point on the horizon, the better shall we be equipped for the strife to which we are called to-day. It has been said, and with truth, that the intellectual conflict which the Church must wage to-day is no longer with this or that heresy; it is no more Catholicity *versus* Protestantism, but Christianity *versus* Paganism. It is Church or no Church; it is faith or infidelity. Modern paganism rejects the Holy Scriptures as the inspired Word of God, scoffs at tradition, despises the fathers, doctors, and theologians of the Church, and takes its stand on reason alone. It knows nothing of the Supernatural, will have nothing of it, rules it out of all discussion. But the Sacramental System is the exhibition, the application, the realization of the Supernatural to men; and the wider its influence is felt, the farther its salutary machinery extends, the more sensibly must the Supernatural be felt and known among men.

A few words in conclusion. We have been looking upon the lesser lights in the firmament of the Church; we have not yet fixed our eyes upon the greater orbs which shine there. It is like watching the Pleiades rising through the mellow shade ere descrying the glorious beacon-fire of Jupiter, or the lamps of great Orion blazing through the night. But even so, how wonderful, how precious, are these minor sacraments! What help do they continually minister, what cheer, what joy do they bring to the children of the covenant! By them, as the instruments of God the Holy Ghost, the little ones are made strong in the Lord and in the power of His might; man and woman are bound together by a power even greater than their mutual love, and strengthened by a gift which hallows and sanctifies their wedded life, and makes the home a sacred inclosure, guarded by good angels, and beautiful as a garden of the Lord ; earnest young spirits, in the strength of opening manhood, take up the cross to bear it after Jesus, with the assurance that a strength above their own is given by the laying on of pastoral hands, for the work of the ministry, for the edifying of the Body of Christ ; souls in the grief of penitence or the agony of remorse, in the clouded hours of the mortal day and at the coming of the death-thraw, are comforted and upheld by the clear and cheerful words: "Be of good cheer, thy sins are forgiven thee!" Who can tell how far these streams of mercy flow through the careful, sorrowful world, what wealth of blessing they carry to the habitation of men! It is hard for one who comprehends the subject to understand how men can consent to deprive themselves of this abundant outflow of spiritual refreshment, harder to imagine what we should do without it. The harmonies of nature, the music of the sphered heavens above us, breathe through these mysterious ordinances as winds through the chords of a lute. Everything bespeaks reparation, restoration, the recovery of something lost, the prophecy of something yet more satisfying to come hereafter. Beautiful, indeed, is the world, as the work of God; darkening here and there, no doubt, under deep and solemn shadow, while yet that very shadow adds effect and brilliancy to the rays reflected from the Fount of light perpetual: but when is the world, the created universe, so beautiful as when we see all through it the golden threads, the silvery cords, the broidered work of a divine and sacramental life? "Two worlds are ours," as Keble says, the outer and the inner, and the outer is but the portal through which we pass to the more glorious things within. At each successive stage of mortal pilgrimage we find ourselves in touch with some mysterious power; at every step are we met by something which discloses God and stamps on us a fresh impression and draws us forward, and ever nearer to the unseen. Such is the use of those lesser ordinances, which seem so arranged as to hallow the morning, the noonday, the evening, to fit into the several relations of man to his fellow men, to help him through the rough places, to lead him on,

> " O'er moor and fen, o'er crag and torrent, till
> The night is gone "

Such is their use, and such the use of the hundred more of the same class, though of inferior grade, by which, as by a sign-language, our Father addresses His children. A life ordered on a plan like this must be, upon the whole, one of joy and peace. It is a good thing to know that we are not thrown back on ourselves; that we must not starve from all that the heart desires; that we shall not go unfed, uncomforted, unhouselled, through and out of this world; that we need not make our journey by a bitter path of straitness, leanness, and misery, without helper or Saviour, without sign to faith, or certain assurance, or gleam of spiritual glory from the forms of a godless, soulless creation. Joyful, indeed, must be he who sees through the outer and reads within; who finds God's image and superscription on all that we touch and all that touches us; who feels Him coming forth, through darkness, and making that darkness as clear as the day.

> "Two worlds are ours, 'tis only sin
>   Forbids us to descry
> The mystic heaven and earth within,
>   Plain as the sea and sky
>
> Thou who hast given me eyes to see
>   And love this sight so fair,
> Give me a heart to find out Thee,
>   And read Thee everywhere."

IV.

HOLY BAPTISM.

LECTURE IV.

HOLY BAPTISM.

To attempt a full and satisfactory treatment of the subject of Holy Baptism in a lecture of an hour's length would be to undertake what is beyond the power of man. The Oxford Movement, as it is commonly called, was an instance of the recovery of a Church from lethargy and weakness, through faith in her own divine origin, and the reassertion of her rights as a branch of the Catholic family. That movement commenced, as was natural, with the reaffirmation of the principle of Apostolic Succession, as vital to the proof of legitimacy, it proceeded with the restatement of the doctrines of grace and their sacramental application. About the year 1835, when the movement was in successful progress, Dr Pusey prepared what is described by Dean Church as "perhaps the most elaborate treatise on Baptism that has yet appeared in the English language."* It came out in

---

* "The Oxford Movement," p 119

three parts, in the "Tracts for the Times," forming, in the second edition, a volume of four hundred pages. Let a man look through that volume, crammed as it is with quotations from Holy Scripture, the Fathers, the Liturgies, and the writings of all kinds of dissenters and heretics, ancient and modern, and he will form a just idea of the breadth and importance of the subject now before us, and the impossibility of doing it justice in the time at my command. I must limit myself to saying a few things, as concisely as possible, on the first of the two great Sacraments of the Gospel, in its relation to the Incarnation, and its place in the extension of the benefits thereof to the human family.

And, first, be this observed, that Holy Baptism is declared by the Church to be "generally necessary to salvation." The statement is made, of course, on the authority of Christ, who said, "He that believeth and is baptized shall be saved;"* and "except a man be born of water and the Holy Ghost he cannot see the kingdom of God."† This sacrament, as we understand the case, is the instrument whereby men are grafted into the vine, and

---

* St Mark, xvi. 16. † St John, iii 5.

placed in direct and personal relation to Christ, the Second Adam. In baptism they are made "members of Christ, children of God, and inheritors of the kingdom of heaven,"* relations not held before the administration of the rite. They are "buried with Christ in baptism, wherein also they are risen with Him."† The moment of baptism is, for them, that of a new birth into a life in God. Where that sacrament may be had, no man is, or can be, in Christ till he be baptized. These are very simple statements; they constitute the first lessons taught to the children of the Church; they form the basis of Christian education. And yet, notwithstanding this rudimental cast, they are statements which it is all-important for us at this particular time to reiterate, and teach with diligence, because the drift of popular thought is against them. To watch that drift is the duty of the Clergy of this Church and of all who desire to educate on her lines; and I think that there is no more curious or interesting subject of consideration at present than the persistency of the tenets of Pelagius and his followers, and the fascination exerted by them on the modern mind. The Pelagian her-

---

* Catechism in Book of Common Prayer † Col. ii 12

esy has a vitality unexampled in the history of religious error; its strength to-day may be seen in the popularity of such ideas as these—that every human being, from the fact that he is man, is already in vital union with Christ, from the fact that Christ is man also; that the immediate effect of the incarnation was to make Christ immanent in all nations and in every individual of the race. This Christo-Pantheism—for it cannot be uncharitable to designate it by that title—is manifestly without support in the Scriptures; it is contradictory to the entire tenor of the teaching of the apostles, and irreconcilable with their acts; it is equally irreconcilable with what we are taught in the Church as to the need and the grace of Holy Baptism. For among the first principles of Church teaching are these, that in us is an innate fault and corruption; that men are unable by any efforts of their own to help, or raise, or save themselves out of that natural state of depression; that fallen nature has within it no recuperative power, till God touches it from outside, and that, generally, no man can be in Christ except he be born again of water and the Holy Ghost. These statements are principles of the doctrine of Christ, and a part of the foundation of the Christian Religion, and we may add, as the result of observation, that wherever they are denied the tendency soon becomes evident to change religion into a philosophy and to deny the divine and supernatural elements which constitute its vital force.

It is proposed to consider the gifts of Holy Baptism under the three heads of

1. *Forgiveness of Sins.*
2. *Regeneration.*
3. *Illumination.*

And, first, of the Forgiveness of Sins. That this is granted in Holy Baptism to every duly qualified recipient, is an article of the Christian faith. "I acknowledge one baptism for the forgiveness of sins." And here we come at once upon the distinction between Sin Original and Sin Actual. It has been, and is, the practice of the Catholic Church to admit infants to Holy Baptism. She does this on the line of the article in the Creed, on the ground that there is in them a sin which needs and receives forgiveness; for, if it were not so, it would follow that in places where the Church was settled and dominant, and at times when adult baptism was the exception, and infant baptism the rule, the article of the Creed just referred to was without significance. The Church teaches that "all men are conceived and born in sin;"* the words are the first which the minister utters in his official character whenever an infant is presented for baptism; the act of so presenting is justified and explained by the Church's estimate of the child's natural and actual condition; to speak of a sinless, spotless infant is to describe what has never existed on the earth since the hour of the Fall, save once, in Bethlehem of Judea, when Christ our Lord was born "Original, or birth sin, is the fault and corruption of the nature of every man that is naturally engendered of the offspring of Adam . . . and in every person born into this world it deserveth God's wrath and damnation."† To mend that fault is God's first work, a work which must be done before anything else can be done. It is a fault in the nature; it has nothing individual or personal in it at first; it is not to be confused with act, will, or character; the sufferer is not responsible. And yet it is a difficulty calling for serious attention—an obstacle which must be somehow disposed of. The best time to deal with it is at the birth of the child into the world, for then no bar is interposed to the act of the physician and surgeon

---

* Offices of Baptism in Book of Common Prayer.
† Article IX

of the soul. The state of infancy is, to the soul
under treatment, what the etherized condition is to
a patient undergoing an operation—the subject,
when passive and unconscious, is completely under
command. So with divine grace in this sacrament;
the fault in our nature is the thing to be corrected,
helped, or removed; wherever that fault exists the
sacrament is required, and may be effectual; it will
be effectual unless man place some obstacle in the
way. A child, as inheritor of the trouble common
to the race, is a proper subject for treatment; a
child, having as yet committed no actual sin, is
then best fitted for sacramental absolution as being
unable by thought, word, or act to stay the effectual working of the Holy Ghost. So do we think,
and so believe, of the "one baptism for the forgiveness of sins." In that sacrament original sin is forgiven, wherever it exists; in infants, of course,
because there is in them none other to forgive;
and if the subject be of riper years, his actual sins,
committed prior to baptism, are also washed away.
Thus the doctrine of Holy Baptism contains the
refutation of the error of those who deny the original corruption of human nature. It is not to be
regarded as a mere external washing, similar to the
ablutions practised by the Jews and other ancient

people; nor is it a mere initiatory rite; but it is a power of the world to come. It witnesses, first, to the absolute need of cleansing ere any one can come to the presence of God; it witnesses, secondly, to the atoning work of Christ, who, by the shedding of His precious blood, and by His application of the merits of that blood, so cleanses the soul of the sinner. With singular fitness is the sign of the Cross made in the administration of that sacrament, since baptism refers us to the death on Calvary, and derives its vitality from that sacrificial act. To deny the strength and power of sin is to take all serious meaning out of this sacrament; it seems to serve thenceforth no purpose sufficiently important to justify its retention; if retained, it is, perhaps, as a dead form from which the spirit has passed away.

Secondly, baptism is "a sign of Regeneration or new birth;" thereby, "as by an instrument, men are grafted into the Church," which is the Body of Christ.* Here again we tread on ground worn by many a bitter controversy, and deeply tracked by the feet of combatants; but it is a comfort to reflect that the battle, though long, did not termi-

---

* Article XXVII

nate in a doubtful issue. There is no reasonable ground of doubt, that in the Prayer-book Offices for the Ministration of Baptism, regeneration is put foremost as a baptismal gift; the fact cannot be concealed; right or wrong, that is the teaching of the Church. The notorious Gorham case, though its immediate effect was to sustain the clique who denied regeneration in baptism, was, in its ultimate result, a blessing to the Church; as has been well observed:

"The storm of controversy raised by that case so cleared the atmosphere of the clouds by which the subject of baptismal regeneration had been obscured, as practically to put an end to all discussion about it, and a later generation wonders how such a discussion could ever have arisen when the language of Holy Scripture and of the Prayer-book is now seen to be so singularly plain and dogmatic "*

The change to which we apply the name of regeneration is not to be confounded with conversion, or alteration of any kind in disposition, mind, will, or heart. It goes far deeper, down to the roots of the being; it implants a spiritual seed from which the whole spiritual life, including the spiritual body which man shall wear eternally, is to be evolved.

---

* Blunt's "Dictionary of Sects, Heresies, etc," p 198

As Dr. Pusey says:

"One may then define Regeneration to be that act whereby God takes us out of our relation to Adam, and makes us actual members of His Son, and so His sons, as being members of His Ever-Blessed Son, and if sons, then heirs of God through Christ (Gal. iv. 7.) This is our new birth, an actual birth of God, of water, and the Spirit, as we were actually born of our natural parents; herein then, also, are we justified, or both accounted and made righteous, since we are made members of Him who is alone righteous; freed from past sin, whether original or actual; have a new principle of life imparted to us, since, having been made members of Christ, we have a portion of His life, or of Him who is our life; herein we have also the hope of the resurrection and of immortality, because we have been made partakers of His resurrection, have risen again with Him." (Col. ii. 12.)

A man has no more to do with his second birth into Christ, regarded in its character as a divine act wrought on him, than he had to do with his birth from his mother's womb. We are here directly in front of the mystery of the Incarnation and its extension to us. There was a first Adam; there is a second. From the first we are descended *carnaliter;* from him, our common ancestor, we inherit that disordered constitution with which we are born into the world; in that first Adam we all die; for as his descendants we are become subject to the law of sin in our members, and to the wage and penalty of sin, which is death. But there is a Second Adam; and what we lost by descent from the first is made up to us, and more than made up, in the Second. God, by His law in grace, makes us members of the Second, as by the law of nature we are members of the first. Regeneration is God's gift to man, in the sacrament of the new birth. For then we receive the germ of a new and immortal life; we are born again, into another family and household; we come under new conditions, we enter into a new environment; we have a new Father, we are set free from the law of sin and death. The analogy between the two ancestries is complete and exact. If the descent from the earthly ancestor be a real and practical thing, not less real and practical is the relation to the heavenly Head. It is not an affair of suppositions, metaphors, and figures of speech, but a vital reality. This change in the nature—not in the individual, and in the state—not in the character, is what the Church means, in declaring of every person duly baptized that he is thereby regenerate. Regeneration would not be regeneration, if effected by ourselves; it is brought about by God the Holy Ghost, the Lord and Giver of life. It is accomplished, not by man, in the use of any power of his own, nor could it be, for the condition in which he comes into the world deprives him of the ability to make himself over on this wise; not by man, nor by blood, nor by the will of the flesh; not by wish for betterment, nor by faith in himself; not by struggle and strife and aspirations, but by the power and grace of God the Holy Ghost. To mark that fact more distinctly, and to keep the man, at the outset of this new career, on the line of his whole mundane existence, in which, as we are never to forget, life comes down from without and not from within, it is accomplished by sign and symbol, by uttered word, by mention of the name of God, the Three and One, and by the use of an element of the natural world, "sanctified to the mystical washing away of sin;" and thus human nature, as realized in the person of one poor suffering and dying creature, is brought into union with that same human nature as realized in power, glory, and eternal life, in the person of the Son of God. This is to be born anew of water and of the Spirit; and thus is the Incarnation extended to us, man by man, in the sacrament of baptism.

I believe that this doctrine is in perfect accord with the best scientific thought of the day, with sound philosophy, and with the theology of the

Church, and that it will receive fresh confirmation from study in those departments.

Holy Baptism is, for the individual, the beginning, the starting-point, in his new creation; the *agōn*, the battle, has not yet come on, nor the time when he must do for himself. The power of the sacramental system lies first in God, in nature, and in the constituted order of things before it reaches men. It is not an evolution in ourselves, nor an outcome of our effort; and nothing is more distinctly narrow and contracted than the idea that regeneration and conversion must be one and the same thing, for that is as much as to say that it is really the man who regenerates himself.

To quote again from our great master.

"No change of heart, or of the affections, no repentance, however radical, no faith, no life, no love, come up to the idea of this 'birth from above,' it takes them all in, and comprehends them all, but itself is more than all, it is not only the creation of a new heart, new affections, new desires, and, *as it were*, a new birth, but is an *actual* birth from above or from God—a gift coming down from God, and given to faith, through Baptism, yet not the work *of* faith, but the operation *of* 'water and the Holy Spirit,' the Holy Spirit giving us a new life in the fountain opened by Him, and we being born therein *of* Him, even as our Blessed and Incarnate Lord was, according to the flesh, born *of* Him in the Virgin's womb,

Faith and repentance are the conditions on which God gives it, water, sanctified by our Lord's baptism, the womb of our new birth, love, good works, increasing faith, renovated affections, heavenly aspirations, conquest over the flesh, its fruits in those who persevere, but it itself is the gift of God, a gift incomprehensible, and not to be confounded with or restrained to any of its fruits (as a change of heart, or conversion), but illimitable and incomprehensible, as that great mystery from which it flows, the Incarnation of our Redeemer, the Ever-Blessed Son of God."

Science here comes to the aid of Catholic theology and confirms her statements. Life can only come by contact with life. Life must come from outside, there is no such thing as spontaneous generation. It is so with natural life; it is so with spiritual life. It is not the man who makes himself to live; who evolves himself out of matter, and so becomes the author of his own act. Even so, in the case of the soul, to make it alive, it must be touched from without with life from above. The source of that life is the glorified humanity of the Son of God. It is a free gift to us, granted complete, without cooperation or agency of ours. It is a grace, a power, a vital germ, a new force, conveyed to us by Holy Baptism, as by an instrument and channel of importation. To fail to see this, and to insist, as has been done, that the work begins in the man himself, and that spiritual life is the result of his prevenient action, is to take a position not only destructive of the leading principle in Catholic theology, but also inconsistent with the laws of life in the natural and moral spheres.

The Holy Scriptures speak of men as being buried with Christ in baptism; raised with Christ in that sacrament; then and thereby planted in the likeness of Christ's death, freed from the law of sin, made complete in Him, and seated with Him in heavenly places. These expressions indicate, apparently, the presence and action of some unknown power, some unearthly force, something out of the height, coming down upon men, working incredible change, conveying supernatural gifts and blessings; gifts which men are competent to receive at any age, and do receive, to the good of the soul, if they place no bar in the way. Children, as has been observed, can place no bar in the way, from the very nature of the case, and therefore infant baptism is the normal and perfect illustration of our subject. Adults may hinder or prevent its operation by ignorance, by indifference, by want of due preparation; to their own part must they look, to their duty must they be urged by their spiritual guides; but the lot of the children is happier, and of such is the kingdom of heaven. Then, when the life has been imparted, the child having been extricated from the womb of its native condition and brought into the communion of the Body of Christ, we look for the fruits of the regenerating spirit in the life of faith, the turning consciously to God, the works of righteousness, the processes of conversion and progressive sanctification. These are the aftergrowth; the seed was sown by the Divine Sower, and this is the harvest. To fail to see these distinctions is a calamity. It is a fatal error to confuse God's great sacramental gift of regeneration with the conditions required of an adult who has not yet come to the holy sacrament, or with the fruits expected to follow where that prevenient grace has been shed forth upon the soul.

"Baptismal regeneration," says Dr Pusey, "as connected with the Incarnation of our Blessed Lord, gives a depth to our Christian existence, an actualness to our union with Christ, a reality to our sonship to God, an interest in the presence of our Lord's glorified Body at God's right hand, a joyousness amid the subduing of the flesh, an overwhelmingness to the dignity conferred on human nature, a solemnity to the communion of saints, who are the fulness of Him who filleth all in all, a substantiality to the indwelling of Christ, that to those who retain this truth the school which abandoned it must needs appear to have sold its birthright"*

There is yet a third gift to man in this first sacrament of the Gospel; it is that of Illumination. In two well-known passages in the Epistle to the Hebrews the inspired writer, referring to the baptized, styles them the illuminated † The term was constantly used in the first age of Christianity. Holy Baptism was spoken of as "the illumination," and the illuminated were the baptized. The times for baptism, and the rites and ceremonies connected with its administration, suggested the same idea. Epiphany, Easter, and Whitsuntide were deemed the seasons fittest for the great ordinance, they who came to it were clad in white and carried lighted lamps or tapers in their hands. At the baptism of the younger Theodosius, we are told, there was a splendid procession; all wore white and carried lights, so that the street appeared to be covered with snow, and the stars seemed to have left the heavens and to be moving in a flood of radiance upon the earth. The name, the symbolism and ritualism, the accessories, tell one clear story; they place the gifts of Holy Baptism before

---

* "Tracts for the Times," No 67
† Heb. vi 4, x 32, φωτισθεντας, φωτισθεντες

us in another aspect ; they bear on the trying question of reason and faith. We cannot for a moment suppose that our ancient fathers were thus engaged in childish play and empty ceremonies ; they meant something, and by those significant proceedings they declared a momentous truth.

Light is the medium of vision; by means of it objects become perceptible to the organs of sight. The organ of sight and the medium of vision are not the same ; eyes are of no use without light; in the dark the most perfect eye sees nothing. So, then, light is not the thing which sees, nor is it the object seen, but a medium, a go-between, a somewhat central between the observer and the thing observed, but not to be confused with either. And illumination is the act of supplying light ; the shedding abroad of that by means of which things become visible which were invisible before. When, therefore, the sacred writers and the primitive Christians called baptism illumination, and spoke of the baptized as illuminated, they expressed a profound truth in the use of that word.

We discern between material light, intellectual light, and spiritual light. There is the light of this world, with the aid whereof the bodily eye discerns the material objects around us. There is an intellectual light, derived from education and culture, by which the human reason and understanding sees and apprehends the subjects of thought. After these there is another light. It is not material light; it is not the light of reason. These avail in the natural world and in the world of intellect. But above these there is a higher world; a world inaccessible to man in his own powers, a world where things cannot be touched, investigated, or seen by the eye of the body or the eye of the mind. Light is needed before man can make out what is there, or gain any certain information concerning the mysteries and wonders of that higher sphere. The light needed for that purpose is the illumination received in Holy Baptism, a divine gift from God to the eye of the soul; a medium of vision in spiritual things by which the spirit of man, which is in him, becomes able to see the things of the Spirit of God.

The parallels appear to be complete, the analogies perfect. As a denizen of the material world man has the eye of the body, and the light whereby to use it, and thus he sees, and that is the natural light. In the intellectual sphere man has the reason, and the subjects which are apt to its powers and within its range; but the reason is useless till it be provided with its proper light—a light derived from training and study, shining all about us in modern civilization, demanding fidelity to it, and capable of increase or diminution, according to the right use or the abuse of the intellectual powers. In his relations to the spiritual world man has the reason and the understanding as before, but now he needs another light, apt to study and discovery in that higher sphere. Body, mind, and spirit, however perfect in themselves, must remain in ignorance of their proper objects, unless light be given to each whereby to see. The eye may be perfect, and yet absolutely useless for want of natural light. The mind may be acute and clear, and yet a man may live and die in ignorance, for want of knowledge and education. The spirit, though capable of seeing divine truth, and acquainting itself with God and all holy mysteries, may remain in darkness and error, like that of the pagan, heretic, and unbeliever, because it lacks, or has rejected, the illumination whereby God shows the spirit the things concerning himself. That light comes *to* us, not *from* us; it is light from a world above; it is shed abroad in the heart by God the Holy Ghost; it is conveyed to the soul, together with the remission of sin and the gift of regeneration, in the sacrament ordained to that end by Him who said: " I am the Light of the world."

This is the Catholic doctrine of Holy Baptism. In it man receives a new spiritual sense, given for certain purposes, for supernatural ends. He has the material senses; the intellectual powers; and now a spiritual faculty, whereby he is able to discern truths not accessible to the senses in their common use, nor to the reason in its proper action. He is thus equipped for every relation and every duty. He can know the world of nature, the world of thought, and the world of grace. He is provided with what he needs, as tenant of many spheres. But greatest of all these gifts is the last Thereby he sees what the eye cannot see, what the ear cannot hear, what the intellect cannot comprehend; things beyond the reach of touch or taste or visual perception, things more important than aught else to him as heir of immortality. And in the use of this new power he gains knowledge to be had in no other way; not by experiment, not by argument, not by logical demonstration, but a knowledge imparted through a light flashing in upon the soul he knows not how. This is the double gift to man in the illumination at the font: outside, a broad medium of revealed truth and doctrine, summed up in the Catholic creed, inside, an illuminative gift and spiritual faculty enabling him to see it and to live thereby.

It is hardly necessary to add that these faculties depend for their maintenance on proper use. Men may ruin their eyes by careless and improper exercise or neglect; they may ruin their intellectual powers by abuse; they may deprive themselves of their spiritual sight by neglect, self-conceit, moral cowardice, and sin. Nor is it necessary to observe that, in the case of adults, repentance and faith are the conditions antecedent to the right reception of this holy sacrament, and that the gift to every man shall be less or greater according to his conscientiousness in the use thereof. But it must be always remembered that the repentance, the faith, the subjective condition, are *not* the baptismal gift. That gift is God's; it cometh down from the Father of lights; our part is to make ready for its reception as well as we can, and, having received, to keep it thereafter safe from profanation, misuse, and loss.

I wish now to speak briefly about a remarkable phase in the office for the Ministration of Baptism *" Sanctify this water to the mystical washing away of sin."* The words may recall to your minds what was said in a previous lecture on the relation of the sacramental system to the order of the visible creation. And here I wish I had time to read to you, by way of exposition of this part of my subject, that portion of Dr. Pusey's volume on Holy Baptism in which, in treating of the wonder of the Christian miracle and the simplicity of the outward sign, he has brought together, with marvellous patience and fulness, the instances in the Old and New Testaments in which this element of water has been used by Almighty God in His dealings with men, and the deductions of holy writers from these acts of divine Providence. There is a wealth, a fulness in these illustrations, of which every mind and heart imbued with the spirit of sacramental Christianity must feel the force and beauty. Beginning with that epoch of the creative day when the Spirit of God moved upon the face of the waters; following the course of the four rivers which went out of Eden; we come to the Old Testament types: the flood; the wells of the patriarchs, which the Philistines stopped with earth, the well of water shown to Hagar; the passage of the Red Sea; Elim, with its twelve wells and its threescore and ten palm-trees; the smitten rock, the water out of the well of Bethlehem, by the gate; the cleansing of Naaman in Jordan; the transit of Elijah through that river on his way home to God. Then we take up the prophecies, reading in Isaiah of the waters breaking out in the wilderness and streams in the desert;* in Ezekiel, of his vision of the holy waters,† in Zechariah, of the fountain opened to the house of David and to the inhabitants of Jerusalem for sin and for uncleanness‡ And so we pass through the veil into the days of Christ, and read of the well of Samaria, and the water changed to wine at Cana of Galilee, and the waters of baptism applied by John, the forerunner of the Lord, and of the water which, mingled with blood, flowed from the side of Christ. The office of the types was a great one; they prefigured the coming of an hour when to this element of water was to be imparted a sanctification which should lift it out of the order of natural substances and natural uses, and give it a mystical and miraculous efficacy. We find in the old liturgies the distinct recognition of this sanctifying and glorifying of that element which, however common and humble, has now acquired a more than natural or material-force, being made an instrument to join

---

* Isa xxxv. 6 † Ezek xlvii. 1-12.
‡ Zech xiii 1

man to the Incarnate Lord. The recognition of this mysterious power, now imparted to it by the power of the Holy Ghost, is not an individual opinion nor a fanciful notion, nor a passage in a romantic dream. It was found in the ancient Church; it is in every baptismal liturgy of the old time; it was retained among the Lutheran bodies which remained faithful to the ancient tradition; it is preserved among us inviolably by that remarkable phrase in our office. And it cannot be doubted that the thought of the strange connection between the work of God in nature and His work in grace was in the minds of the fathers, and that they found one of the clearest illustrations of it in the institution of this holy sacrament.

"There is in the ancient Church what by moderns would be condemned as realism or materialism or mysticism. Their view seems to have been of this sort Since God had appointed the use of water for baptism, there must have been an appropriateness in it which there was in no other element, that there was an analogy between His physical and moral creation, and that not only imaginative but real, that in forming the physical, He had respect also to the purposes which He designed in His moral creation, and imparted to the physical agent properties corresponding to its moral uses, that in His earlier dispensations He had regard to the latter, and not only taught man beforehand what should be, but in a manner, by employing His creature in the subordinate office of the former, imparted to it a fitness to serve in the latter and greater Something of this sort, as derived from the ancient Church, is acknowledged by our own, that the baptism of our Lord 'sanctified water to the washing away of sin,' *i e*, at the least, our Lord's baptism in Jordan imparted to the whole element of water a capacity of becoming the instrument of washing away sin, which, apart from His baptism, it would not have had."*

With a brief reference to the opposition made to the doctrine of Holy Baptism as held in the Catholic Church, I shall bring this lecture to an end. Why should there be such obstinate resistance to a teaching so profound, so consoling, so sublime? Why should men substitute for it the initiatory-rite theory, the bare-form notion? How shall we explain the position of the Anabaptist, who insists on immersion, but denies any spiritual efficacy or sacramental grace in the rite? What shall be thought of the disciples of the Gorham school, whose contention was, that regeneration must occur before or after baptism, but could not possibly occur at the time of administration? These phenomena are merely instances of the power of the doctrine and the force of the recoil

---

* "Pusey on Baptism," pp 286, 287

from its claim on reverence and faith. To allege that God grants to men, in an exterior rite, remission of sin, regeneration, and illumination, is to antagonize three classes of free-thinkers on religion. That baptism confers remission of sin, original and actual, must be denied by the Pelagian, who thinks there is no such thing as original sin, and minimizes our need of divine grace. That baptism is generally necessary as a means of grafting men into the Body of Christ is denied by the neo-Pantheist, who holds that all men are already in Christ, because He has taken on Him the nature common to us all. Finally, to say that in Holy Baptism a light is given to the mind and spirit, enabling us to discern things not to be seen in our natural condition, is to affront the philosophic Rationalist, who relies on reason alone for the discovery and investigation of truth. A doctrine which thus deals its blow at a trinity of errors as old as the human race itself, must expect the reception which it meets with in the Pelagian, Pantheistic, and Rationalistic schools. No one imbued with the principles of those schools can say, sincerely, and without reservation: " I ACKNOWLEDGE ONE BAPTISM FOR THE REMISSION OF SINS."

Thirty years have passed away since the notorious Gorham controversy agitated, or it may almost be said, convulsed, the Church. The salutary effect of the clearing of the air and the settling of the mind of the community on the subject involved, has been long perceived and is gratefully acknowledged. Since that day other questions have come to the front, and the minds of men have been drawn off in other directions. But the doctrine which was then successfully vindicated, as being unquestionably that which is taught in our offices, has lost no whit of its importance; and that great sacrament is still, as always, the foundation of the Church system, and the bulwark against all heresies, old and new. With the passing of the years, the pendulum swings back along its arc, till now, amid the din of voices, the denial of sin and its results, the extravagant laudation of humanity, the determined resistance to authority, and the late claim to the natural birthright of every man to identification with Christ as a member of His Body, without the aid of rite, sacrament, or instrumental means of any sort, we have reached the point at which we see plainly the necessity of reaffirming and maintaining against all comers, the old positions regarding Holy Baptism and its threefold gift; to the end that men may be brought within the covenant of grace, and that Christ may regain His hold on the multitude who, having no faith in the Gospel, and no individual relation to His Body the Church, are as a flock scattered abroad upon the mountains, and practically without Him in the world.

V.

HOLY COMMUNION.

LECTURE V.

HOLY COMMUNION.

IF it be deemed a task beyond the power of man to speak fully, in a lecture such as this, of Holy Baptism, what can be done when we come to the greatest of all sacraments? Who, indeed, is worthy to speak of that Rite which has the first claim on love and devotion; in which are the highest height, the deepest depth, the broadest breadth; for which an adequate title was sought in vain by holy men of old; which is life and joy with peace to them that receive it worthily, but misery and death to those who profane it? On his knees might one desire to write on this subject what it should be given him to say.

For now we are come to a strangely exact illustration of the function of the Sacramental System as an Extension of the Incarnation; this is especially the ordinance wherein men, living in Christ, are fed out of the fulness of the Humanity now borne by Him, and progressively fitted for the heavenly realm. For here " we spiritually eat the flesh of Christ and drink His blood; we dwell in Christ, and Christ in us; we be made one with Christ, and Christ with us." And so, first, I shall endeavor to show that the Mystery of His Holy Incarnation, from the fourfold point of view in which it invites our study, is so reflected in this great sacrament, that terms apt to either seem at once to fit the other. Christ, present to us by His indwelling in the nature common to us all, becomes present in a still more marvellous way in this ordinance. He is so realized to us therein, that what is said of Him outside this Sacrament may be said, word for word, of the Sacrament itself. In its relation to Him, and in its relation to us in Him, let us proceed to consider it; not in a controversial temper, but rather as citizens rejoicing in the glory of the kingdom, and counting the riches of their inheritance among the saints. It may be remarked in passing, that the dreadful unreality of modern religion, inaccurately styled Christian, seems to have come as a Nemesis on unbelief in the Sacramental Presence of Christ in His Church, and on the persistence with which men contradict the words of the Master, saying, "This is *not* His Body, this is *not* His Blood," though He affirmed of each its verity and its truth.

In the sacrament of the altar we are brought to

the point where the natural and the supernatural come most closely together. To the eye of faith, the Christian Altar appears like a headland jutting into a vast and open sea; waves roll in from the eternal space, to strike upon the shores of time. It is a mirror of all truth, human and divine. It has a twofold aspect, being Sacrifice and Sacrament in one; it is each in turn, in complete and matchless perfection; it is the pure and unbloody Offering, the heavenly Feast. It represents the work of the world's High Priest, now going on above; it brings Him, verily and indeed, into our midst with holy gifts. It is pictorial, it is practical; a grand action is displayed and accompanied, a work of immediate necessity is carried on. As Christ stands at the mercy-seat on high, appearing before His Father as our Mediator and Redeemer, and making intercession for us, so stands the priest as His representative, offering on earth the same oblation which Christ offers in heaven, and sending up the liturgical prayer. Christ promised to feed men with His Flesh and Blood, adding, "Whosoever eateth My Flesh and drinketh My Blood hath everlasting life, and I will raise him up at the last day." * Here,

---

* St. John, vi 54.

in Holy Communion, He meets His faithful children for that purpose, and, under forms selected from the natural world, and hallowed and blessed for a supernatural effect, He gives them what He promised. In its double aspect, as sacrifice, as sacrament, this Rite is first in dignity, and, in power, most efficient. Nothing can be set before it, nor can care, pains, or cost be too great in realizing it for all that it is to our devotion and faith. And this, above all, must we be sure to hold, that it is not ourselves who make it what it is, that it is not our subjective act, nor the moral fitness of the recipient, which gives its reality to that sacrament, and effects the Awful Presence of the Lord therein. Our part is to wait for the Holy Ghost till He come, and, when He has blessed and sanctified the oblation, to draw near with faith, and take the Body and the Blood, feeling that God in Christ is all in all, and that it is He who giveth us the bread that feedeth unto everlasting life.

Let us begin by taking up that invaluable compendium of instruction for our children, which we know so well, and observe how, in its simple yet profound statements and distinctions, the Catechism helps us to take in the idea of the Holy Communion. You all know that the fifth section of the

Catechism was added in 1604, after the Hampton Court Conference, and that its authorship is ascribed to Bishop Overal. Whoever it was that gave it to the Church, he has a claim on our gratitude. As to the sacrament of Holy Baptism, two points are made; there are an outward visible sign or form, and an inward spiritual grace. No hard question is raised as regards the element of water; it is indeed sanctified to a holy use, and it should be reverently disposed of after serving its purpose; but there are no vexatious uncertainties about presences and absences, substances and accidents; it is an instance of the use of an element of the natural order as an instrument whereby, without change in the element, gifts are granted to the soul and spirit of man. But when we pass to the consideration of the Sacrament of the Lord's Supper, the language becomes more ample; the ideas to be presented are more complex, additional phrases are required, and a more detailed description. The elements now used fix our attention, as if some change had passed upon, over, or through them, by which their position in the world of the material and physical had been modified in some wondrous way. We are told, first, of an outward sign; and such we also saw in baptism. But now and next we are told of an inward part or thing signified; to which nothing in the account of baptism corresponds. Finally, we are told of benefits received in the partaking of that Holy Sacrament. The description of the second of the sacraments of the Gospel differs specifically from that of the first. In the one there is a mystery not encountered in the other; the questions and answers in the Catechism make this plain. No Zwinglian would need three terms such as we have here to convey his barren notion of the Holy Communion; to him they would be embarrassing and useless verbiage. But, to tell us the mind of the Church on this sacrament, these words and distinctions are indispensable. They suggest something very strange, and very hard to express. They present a mystery so startling, and so offensive to the natural mind, that dispute has been kept up incessantly about it, ever since the hour in which the Lord announced it to the Jews at Capernaum, and let them go, muttering, as they withdrew, " This is a hard saying: who can hear it?"*

"*Quaenam est pars externa, seu signum Coenae Domini?*

"*Quaenam est pars interna, seu res significata?*

"*Quaenam sunt beneficia quae inde percipimus?*"

---

* St John, vi 60, 66

Three terms are to be considered: the sign, *signum*, the thing signified, *res*, the benefit received, *beneficia*, or *virtus*. There was, undoubtedly, a motive in thus presenting the subject to human thought. The words were not strung together hap-hazard; they were adopted as involving propositions of great interest and importance, and as we study these three words, *signum, res, virtus*, keeping each distinct from the rest, and noting what would happen if the perfect balance among them should be destroyed, we find ourselves substantially going over the ground traversed in our study of the Incarnation of the Son of God, the relations of the two natures in His one Person, and the heresies which for six centuries vexed the Church, indeed, it seems impossible not to be deeply impressed by the correspondence between the two subjects.

First, it is to be noted that these three, the Sign, the Thing signified, and the Benefits conveyed, are distinct and diverse the one from the other, so that no one can be confounded with or substituted for any other without damage to a perfect symmetry in the teaching. The *sacramentum* is not the *res*, the *res* is not the *virtus*. The *sacramentum* and the *res* must not be separated, neither must they be confused; the *sacramentum* must not be annihilated by the *res*, nor must the *res* be thrown away to keep the *sacramentum*. Nor yet should it be supposed that wherever the *sacramentum* and the *res* are, the *virtus* must always be conferred. These distinctions are vital. We see their bearing the moment we place the Catholic Doctrine of the Incarnation and the teaching of the Church about Holy Communion side by side.

You are, of course, familiar with the luminous presentation of the subject of the Incarnation in the 5th Book of the " Ecclesiastical Polity : "

"To gather, therefore, into one sum all that hitherto hath been spoken touching this point, there are but four things which concur to make complete the whole state of our Lord Jesus Christ, His Deity, His Manhood, the conjunction of both, and the distinction of the one from the other being joined in one Four principal heresies there are which have in those things withstood the truth, Arians, by bending themselves against the Deity of Christ, Apollinarians, by maiming and misinterpreting that which belongeth to His human nature, Nestorians, by rending Christ asunder, and dividing Him into two persons, the followers of Eutyches, by confounding in His Person those natures which they should distinguish Against these there have been four most famous ancient general councils the Council of Nice, to define against Arians, against Apollinarians the Council of Constantinople, the Council of Ephesus against Nestorians; against Eutychians the Chalcedon Council. In four words, ἀληθῶς, τελέως, ἀδιαιρετῶς, ἀσυγχύτως, truly, perfectly, indivisibly, distinctly, the first applied to His being God, and the second to His being man, the third to His being of both One, and the fourth to His still continuing in that One both we may fully, by way of abridgment, comprise whatsoever antiquity hath at large handled either in declaration of Christian belief or in refutation of the aforesaid heresies. Within the compass of which four heads I may truly affirm that all heresies which touch but the Person of Jesus Christ, whether they have risen in these later days or in any age heretofore, may be with great facility brought to confine themselves."*

These words of the judicious Hooker may be paraphrased, and with the like precision may it be affirmed that all the heresies which have ever arisen touching the sacrament of the altar are capable of arrangement with reference to the distinction already drawn concerning the *signum*, the *res*, and the *virtus*. In that sacrament may be noted what corresponds to the Deity in Christ, to His Humanity, to the perfect union of the two, and to their distinction the one from the other. There is a teaching which impugns the truth of the outward and visible sign; another, which takes away the

---

* "Ecclesiastical Polity," Book V. liv. 10.

inward part or thing signified ; a third which, while it retains both, divides them the one from the other; and a fourth, which commingles and confuses them. The tenet of Transubstantiation, and that of Consubstantiation ; the notion of a Virtual Presence only, and the idea that this is but a historical memorial of a past and finished transaction; these stand towards the Catholic doctrine of the Holy Sacrament somewhat as the heresies of Arianism, Nestorianism, Apollinarianism, and Eutychianism stand to the Catholic dogma of the Incarnation.

According to Catholic teaching, the sacrament considered in itself is complete, and, so to speak, a *fait accompli*, as soon as the priest has done his part and the Holy Spirit has descended on the oblations. The priest takes the bread; he breaks it and lays his hand thereon, repeating the words of institution ; he takes the cup, and, again repeating the words of the Lord, he lays his hand on it and blesses it; and then, by the power of the Holy Ghost, on the official and solemn utterance of the sacred formula, the sacrament is there before the faithful. Nothing more is needed to its completeness. That completeness consists in the union of the outer and inner perfectly and without confusion. The *signum* remains, in its verity and truth; not a shadow deceptive to the senses, but a reality in the material world. The *res* is there, joined to the *signum*, for holy uses; really and truly present, under the external form; for by the REAL Presence is meant, of course, the presence of the *res*. The sign and the thing signified are both present, at once and together; not as though the sign only were there, while the thing signified, absent and distant, must be realized to each man by his mental act and conscious appropriation. They also abide, notwithstanding their sacramental union, each true to itself; not as though the elements had gone as to their natural substance, and a concrete or conglomerate had taken their place. Even so, we assert that in the mystery of the Holy Incarnation the Deity did not consume the humanity, nor did the humanity fulfil the function of a mere representative and reminder of the absent God; neither was the mystery made to exist in the transmission of grace from far away; nor yet was it a hybrid, neither God altogether nor man altogether, which was beheld in Christ.

I shall now endeavor to justify the statement that the leading errors on the subject of this Holy Sacrament run on parallel lines with the principal heresies which assail the doctrine of the Incarnation. In striving to penetrate what is a profound mystery men have lost the mystery itself; they have confused themselves and their friends with curious and vain distinctions; they have robbed the rite of its claim on our faith, and reduced it to the level of intelligible, or commonplace, transactions And first let us consider the *signum*, and note what mischief has been done by the theory that the outward and visible sign has substantially ceased to exist.

It is essential to a sacrament, as defined by our Church, that each part be there, and that each be true, there is no place for deception and illusion. Now the truth of the *signum* is denied by the tenet of Transubstantiation.

"Transubstantiation (or the change of the substance of bread and wine), in the Supper of the Lord, cannot be proved by Holy Writ, but is repugnant to the plain words of Scripture, overthroweth the nature of a sacrament, and hath given occasion to many superstitions" (Article XXVIII)

And therefore that tenet is rejected by our branch of the Church; and rightly, for all the reasons given. It is not a Catholic doctrine. Certainly it cannot be gathered from the Scriptures, nor from the writings of the fathers of the first six hundred years of the Church. There is a noteworthy fact concerning the statements of those fathers on this subject They have been studied, or rather ransacked, with curious results. Roman controversialists have appealed to them for confirmation of their position that the Body and Blood of the Lord are really present in the Eucharist; and with complete success, for that was unquestionably the view of antiquity. But, on the other hand, Protestant controversialists have appealed to the same fathers, in confirmation of their assertion that the bread and wine, as to their natural substance, continued unchanged after consecration; and with equal success, for a moderate acquaintance with antiquity shows that the fathers held both views, and that many, even in the Roman Church, were with them down to the eleventh and twelfth centuries. Holy Scripture and ancient authors teach the substantial permanence of the elements of bread and wine after consecration. The idea of the annihilation of their substance overthrows the nature of the sacrament, by destroying the *signum*, in its true significance and verity, and taking it out of its place in the world of nature to which it belongs; the sign becomes a deceptive apparition; it is not what the senses assert it to be; it is what the humanity in Christ was to the Docetæ, not a reality, but a shadowy, untrue phantasm.

While men thus lose the truth on one side, others, in combating that error, work themselves into a frame of mind in which they cannot assent to another most important truth essential to a right appreciation of the holy mystery. For though the sign remains unchanged as to its substance, a change does certainly pass upon it; the elements through some mysterious influence become " holy gifts,' and forms under which Christ is present; they undergo a change inexplicable and indefinable; a change on the line where material elements, lifted above their natural uses, are made instrumental to supernatural ends; a change like that which may be expected when the heavens and the earth shall pass away, and there shall be new heavens and a new earth. Such a change, requiring no abdication of their function by the senses, yet stimulating faith to its highest point, is believed in by the devout Catholic; and, in believing it, he is saved from a whirlpool of dilemmas, difficulties, and doubts. He need not vex his soul with subtle questions of substance and accident; he need not enter into a hopeless inquiry what the substance can be which goes completely, while extension, appearance, color, taste, and nutritive properties remain; or whether that deserves the name of substance which stays or flits, exists or does not exist, although the element, as to its natural characteristics, remains unimpaired and unaltered. He has no questions of that kind to settle, who, holding that the elements abide and remain in substantial truth, believes that a mystical change has passed on them, by which they have been lifted into a higher sphere for nobler uses; just as he can conceive how nature, without being annihilated, or replaced by something not itself, may be some time advanced to new conditions, and infused with new powers and capacities, to the glory of God and the good of men.

Next let us consider the error which denies the truth of the sacrament on the side of the inward part or thing signified. By the Real Presence is meant the presence of the *res*. But this, as all know, is denied under various forms of objection and by men of divers sects. The flat denial of the *res* in the sacrament is the characteristic of Zwinglianism: there is in the Lord's Supper a sign only, used to refresh the memory and stimulate the sympathetic nature; it is a memorial feast, and nothing else. This error is in its way the same as that of the Socinians, in whose view Christ was a man, and nothing but a man, having no more deity in or about Him than other men might have who walked with God in their generation and attained to extraordinary holiness. Of this error I repeat what has been said already, that it is one with which our sacramental offices cannot by any straining be made to square. From beginning to end, in their cast, their term of expression, their history, and their natural acceptation they repudiate, they abhor the notion that the Lord's Supper was only a repetition of the feasts previously partaken of by Him and His followers in Galilee and elsewhere, and that it was intended to survive among us merely as an affecting and impressive reminder of His death. Zwinglius is the outlaw of Christendom in his attitude toward the sacramental system, the radical of radicals, the rationalist of rationalists. His opinions, that the Eucharist is a bare commemoration of the death of Christ, and that the bread and wine are mere symbols and tokens to remind us of His Body and Blood, and that Christ is present in the Eucharist only by the contemplation of faith, are directly opposed to Scripture and the general opinion of the fathers, as has been proved a thousand times over. His ideas were disapproved by the Lutherans and Calvinists of his own day; they are disapproved to-day by divines of the Protestant bodies around us.

"Zwinglianism," says Dr Henry Van Dyke, "is essentially *rationalistic* in the evil sense of the word. Its chief effort is to explain away or reduce to a minimum the mystery of the Lord's Supper. It assumes that the theory which is most level to our comprehension, which brings the Holy Supper nearest to a common meal where Christians have sweet fellowship together, and makes it agree most with ordinary human experience, is for that reason nearest to the truth."

Dean Stanley once described this reformer as "the clear-headed and intrepid Zwingle." His clear-headedness was that of a man apparently unable to comprehend the Catholic system, and his intrepidity was that of the thrower of dynamite bombs. He could pull down, he could not build up.

"It is not to be wondered at," says that grave and learned man Bishop William Forbes, in his "Considerationes Modestæ," "that those who have such abject opinions of this most august sacrament as these and other modern innovators, should find nothing in it which they can wonder at. Far otherwise did the pious fathers think and write, who were wont to style it 'this terrible mystery,' and would never think of so great a thing without a sacred and religious awe, viz, because they believed most firmly that he who worthily takes these mysteries of the body and blood of Christ, truly and really takes into himself the body and blood of Christ, but in a certain spiritual, miraculous, and imperceptible manner. The opinion of John Calvin," continues the writer, " is much sounder and more endurable than that of Zwinglius."*

This is undoubtedly true, and it would be offensive and injurious to set the teaching of Calvin and the Westminster Confession on the same level with that of the Swiss radical. Theologians of the higher school in the Presbyterian Church of our own day assert with earnestness their belief in the Real Presence. They entertain a high and spiritual idea of the Lord's Supper, and their devotion puts to shame the carelessness of many among us who boast themselves to be unswerving Catholics. But while we honor their reverent spirit, and believe that they are much nearer to the truth than they suppose, we cannot but except to their use of the term " Real Presence " as descriptive of their belief. The word which seems to us most exactly applicable to their error, as we deem it to be, is " *virtualism;*" they confuse the *res* and the *virtus*, making them one; or, rather, making the *virtus* the inward part and not the *res*. In short, this is the

---

* "Considerationes Modestæ," Vol. II p. 383. In Library of Anglo-Catholic Theology.

doctrine not of the Real Presence but of the Real Absence, or the absence of the *res*. And yet it is not absence in the Zwinglian sense; that system rejects the *res* altogether, except in a historical and memorial way. To the virtualist Christ is present, but in virtue, in power, in a grace flowing forth from Him on the reception of the symbols; but the body and blood, the humanity, remain as far away as ever. To confound the *res* and the *virtus*, as if they were the same, is inevitably to exile and banish the former. It is much the same as to say of Christ that He is God and man indeed, but God in heaven only and not here on earth also; "God with us," not as though the tabernacle of God were now with men, but because He sends forth from His distant abode grace, help, and benediction to those who love Him. This appears to be the idea of the virtualists, if that term may be applied to them. Christ is not present; but the virtue, strength, and spiritual power of Christ are given to men; the body and blood of Christ are not present, nor are they received in the Lord's Supper; but symbols only, which signify the benefits procured unto us by the precious blood-shedding of the Lord, and seal to man the gifts of His passion and death. This theory we are compelled to describe as that of the

Real Absence; the absence of the *res* or thing signified, and it has a strong attraction for those who, while devout and spiritual, attach a great importance to the exercise of the reason and private judgment on the subject of religion. The addiction to rationalistic methods, which is so characteristic of the Protestant mind, renders it difficult for persons of that class to accept any doctrine, unless some kind of account satisfactory to the human understanding can be given; the theory of a virtual as opposed to a real presence meets this desire. It is easy to think, that what makes Christ present is a man's own faith, rather than Christ's word; that He is not in the sacrament, under the forms of bread and wine, but absent, and waiting till faith and love invite Him to enter the house of the soul; and thus a deep and precious spiritual blessing is expected in this reverend ordinance, at the price, however, of an infinitesimally small demand on that faith which believes when it cannot prove, and accepts what is beyond our comprehension. There may be great reverence and great devotion, where this theory of the Presence is held; we do not confound it with naked Zwinglianism, nor fault it as unspiritual; our objection is this, that it lowers the dignity of that holy ordinance, takes the mystery from it, and makes it little less simple and intelligible than the theory of the Memorial Meal. It is, in fact, an explanation, apparently invented to secure from demands on faith. Virtue is supposed to descend from Christ in heaven to men on earth, with the speed and directness of the electric current. A spiritual force, a heavenly power, evoked by our faith and love, concentrated by our obedience, become operative at the spot at which we fulfil the command, this is applied by the Omnipotent Spirit. Such a thing is at once understood; it is easy to grasp; it is *so* easily grasped, that we feel that it can only be a partial truth.

Of the tenet of Consubstantiation, one hardly knows what to say. It is a fair question whether the Lutherans really held it; it was never accepted by them, and certainly did not express their opinion; indeed, there is good reason for supposing that the term was invented by their enemies, with the intention of casting a reproach upon them. The idea of a consubstantiation of the body and blood of Christ with the substance of bread and wine, so that an indescribable amalgam is the result, is both blasphemous and absurd. Reference to it is necessary in order to complete the view of the subject, but I shall not impute so gross, so ridiculous a notion to any man until he has distinctly stated that this is what he believes.

Thus far of the correspondence between the Catholic doctrine of the Incarnation and the doctrine of the Holy Eucharist. Venturing to paraphrase the words of the judicious Hooker, we might say:

That there are four things which concur to make the sacrament complete in itself: the Sign, the Thing signified, the Conjunction of both, and their Distinction. Four principal errors have withstood or obscured the truth: that of Transubstantiation, which denies the permanence of the sign; that of Zwinglianism, which denies the presence of the thing signified; that of Virtualism, which separates the sign and the thing signified, so that the thing is really absent, and only present in virtue and effects; that of Consubstantiation, which so confounds the two that neither retains its reality. And to all these errors we oppose the truth, which accords with the words of Holy Scripture and the statements of the old Catholic fathers; which retains the sign in its substantial integrity while admitting in it a mystical and spiritual change on consecration; which declares the real, true, objective presence of the body and blood of Christ under the forms of bread and wine; which makes the *virtus*, the benefits of the sacrament, a result of its worthy reception, and thus confers on man the fulness of the blessing while withholding him from the presumptuous claim that it is his faith rather than God's act which brings to him his Saviour.

At the risk of becoming tedious, I must repeat that the point on which the whole thing turns is this: that the sacrament of the altar is complete in itself by the act of the Holy Ghost, through the consecrating priest, and that it is so presented as an objective reality to the congregation. Exhibiting the union of a higher and a lower part, each perfect after its own kind, one belonging to the natural order, the other to the supernatural, it is offered to men for their edification and help. When we come to Holy Communion we draw near to a proffered gift of God. Whatever we bring—of faith, of contrition, of the devotion of tears, or of doubt, carelessness, indifference—we neither add to nor detract from the mystery. It is shown to men; they who partake worthily receive the benefits offered, and they who receive unworthily eat and drink to themselves condemnation. That appears to be the simple construction of the words of St. Paul about the danger of not discerning the Lord's body in Holy Communion. How can a man be punished for not discerning what is not before him or present to him at all? It is hard to understand how one can be condemned, cast down, and blasted before a Presence which has not yet been realized to him in that sacrament—for failing to discern what was not there to be discerned. This faith, that the sacrament is constituted by the Word and Holy Ghost, and not by the inner act of a human mind and will, is the safeguard of sacramental doctrine from rationalistic perversion. It has been somewhere said by Mr. Lecky, that of English Christians they are all, more or less, in touch with rationalism, as if it ran through all their theology; and that they can never be satisfied with the Word of God or the decisions of the Church until they have submitted them, as critics and judges, to some tests of their own. However that may be, it is well to know, in this particular matter, where the lines run, and that the one view of the Holy Sacrament which contains the confutation of rationalism is that of the real objective Presence. On that point only is the issue squarely joined between the rationalist and the Catholic.

A few words as to the Holy Sacrament in its sacrificial aspect. It serves, and shall serve to the end of the dispensation, a twofold purpose, as a

Memorial, showing forth the death of the Lord till He come, and as a divine and comfortable feast of life. To complete the subject it would be necessary to go back to the Jewish times; to watch the action of the High Priest on the Day of Atonement, and to compare it with that of Christ in His Passion; to see Him offering the sacrifice of blood outside; passing through the veil, disappearing from sight, and going to the presence of God, there to offer the avails of the sacrifice and make intercession for us. It would be necessary, in the next place, to show the correspondence of the acts of those High Priests with the acts of the Christian priest in celebrating the divine mysteries, and to identify the action, in its profound relations, as one and the same from age to age in the Church of the redeemed. But the time does not suffice for this; nor would that branch of this subject be so fitly considered here, where we are tracing the connection of the Sacramental System with the indwelling of Christ in men. After the sacrifice comes the feast upon the sacrifice, and to this your thoughts have been particularly invited; to this most blessed ordinance, the "Esca Viatorum," the Food of Angels, wherein Christ comes to His faithful, as to those who were with Him on earth in Syria in the days of His flesh. What the Catholic Church believes is this, that He is present with us in Holy Communion. Blessed are they that dwell in Thy house, where the truth is known and received; and blessed are they who, having been fed of Thyself on earth in those holy mysteries, shall eat bread with Thee in the kingdom of God!

I would close this discussion with some words of peace. Of the Holy Eucharist, Archdeacon Freeman says:

"It was confessedly, through long ages of the Church, and is by the vast majority of the Christian world at this hour, conceived to be exceedingly mysterious throughout in its nature and operation, to be no less, indeed, than the highest line of contact and region of commingling between heaven and earth known to us, or provided for us, a border land of mystery where, by gradations baffling sight and thought, the material truly blends with the spiritual and the visible shades off into the unseen, a thing, therefore, which of all events or gifts in this world most nearly answers to the highest aspirations and deepest yearnings of our wonderfully compounded being, while in some ages and climes of the Church it has been elevated into something yet more awful and mysterious. Such an ordinance as this—challenging such a position, claiming and known to claim such powers—could never fail at any period to command the attention, if not the reverence, of thoughtful humanity Drawing towards it the longing vision and engaging, in measure or excess, the faith and affections of some ages and minds, awakening the jealous scrutiny and experiencing the colder construction, or the eager opposition, of others, it would be likely to give rise, in ample measure, to the recorded feelings and judgments of mankind concerning it " *

Bearing in mind the variations to which our author refers, we recall with pain the fact that this august and holy sacrament, instituted by our Lord to be the sign of the unity of His brethren, should have become the subject of contention, an occasion of breaches of charity, and the cause of suspicion and separation. May we not, however, indulge the hope that, notwithstanding our disputes and dissensions, there is a substantial agreement in devotion to our Blessed Lord, as realized, reverenced, or remembered in this memorial of His love for sinners? May we not predict the coming of a happy day when men shall come to that holy ordinance, not with hard questions and in a controversial temper, but with the faith which is the evidence of things not seen and the charity which believeth all things? Let us ask whether the Eirenicon so greatly desired be not the doctrine (as held by the Catholic school in our Anglican Communion) of the Real, Spiritual, Ob-

---

* " Principles of Divine Service," Vol II. Introduction

jective Presence of Christ in that Holy Sacrament? Is there any other view which can harmonize all the rest and remove so many grounds of scruple and objection? The formula seems to meet every demand, except that of the unhappy men by whom the idea of mystery and sacramental grace is stiffly and absolutely rejected. The Presence is real; that saves the thing signified: it is a Spiritual Presence; that bars out material and carnal conceptions: it is an Objective Presence; that defends us from the notion that Christ is with us, or absent, solely according to the force of some mental act on our part. We are already very nigh to those, on the one side, who accept the tenet of transubstantiation, and to those, on the other, who believe only in a virtual presence. What is it that separates us from these earnest believers? The tenet of transubstantiation, erroneous as we deem it, is very widely held through Christendom. It is a question whether transubstantiation, as rejected by us, is the same thing as the transubstantiation now believed in by Latin and Greek Christians; whether the difference in the thoughts of intelligent and liberal men in the three communions under consideration is not so slight as to be somewhat hard to define. Let us consider. On one side it is asserted that the elements remain as to their substance unchanged; on the other, it is asserted that they change in substance, while it is conceded that they remain unchanged in extension, figure, appearance, taste, and physical qualities and properties. What then *is* that substance of which these things are said? Why quarrel about the existence or non-existence of an indefinable somewhat which leaves the elements, in a practical point of view, the same that they were? And why is the gulf impassable between those who say that the elements do not change and those who say that whatever change they undergo it does not involve the five particulars just mentioned? Is not the point too intensely refined, too metaphysical for the mind to grasp? And why should not what is admitted on each side satisfy the other?

Again: as for those devout and earnest souls who come to the Lord's Supper full of faith and love, as to a holy ordinance rich in comfort and blessing, expecting to find help and strength, the virtues and graces of the Redeemer, and a spiritual aid for which they look particularly to that Feast, what is there between us and them? Why need they fear, as though some dreadful thing was to be forced on them in our teaching? One thing, and only one, appears to differentiate between their faith and ours. We are thinking of a Christ present in sacramental sign and under visible forms; they are thinking of the same Christ absent, save in His omnipresent Deity. We ask no hard thing of them in moving them to think of the King as *here*, not *there*. We ask no surrender of the function of the senses as verifiers of the truth of objects in the material world; we do not ask them to localize the Saviour, or to think of Him as inclosed in the elements of bread and wine; the Presence which we ask them to acknowledge is a spiritual Presence, while we tell them that it is not less true, not less real, than it was when He dwelt here in the days of His flesh, not less near than it was in the upper room where he sat surrounded by His disciples, and St. John leaned on his bosom. What fuller joy, what better thing, than to know that the Saviour is thus among us, in truth, and that the tabernacle of God is with men?

And if there be sensitive and anxious souls who fear lest, in insisting so earnestly on the truth of the elements, we may slip out of harmony with the mind of the Church on this subject, we have but to remind them of our faith that the Presence which we believe is objective first before it becomes subjective. This keeps us off the shoal on which so many have gone to wreck, and secures the due payment of all glory and honor to Him who alone worketh great marvels, and maketh weak things strong. The man who firmly holds the objective Presence cannot be out of line with the belief of the ages and the doctrine of the Holy Catholic Church —that word sufficiently announces his position.

Therefore we offer this teaching as the Eirenicon which we seem to need to-day; in the quiet trust that God in His good time will make us to be of one mind in the house, on this as on other subjects. To seek for points of agreement is surely a better work than to dwell, morbidly and gloomily, on differences, some of which may be differences rather about words than things. We are happiest when we labor for peace, though it may be that many who hear thereof make them ready to battle. Be it, day by day, our prayer, for ourselves and all other pilgrims and strangers upon the earth:

"LET THY MERCIFUL EARS, O LORD, BE OPEN UNTO OUR PRAYERS, AND ENLIGHTEN THOU OUR HEARTS WITH THE GRACE OF THY HOLY SPIRIT, THAT WE MAY WORTHILY APPROACH THY HOLY MYSTERIES, AND LOVE THEE WITH AN EVERLASTING LOVE, THROUGH JESUS CHRIST. AMEN."

VI.

THE OUTWARD GLORY AND THE INWARD GRACE.

LECTURE VI.

THE OUTWARD GLORY AND THE INWARD GRACE.

Two things remain to be done before bringing these lectures to a close. We have traversed a field of great extent, in considering the Sacramental System as disclosed in Nature, in man, and in our religion. I wish to say some words, briefly, on its twofold manifestation, externally, in the worship of the Church, and internally, in the life of the soul, and on the development of the seed sown therein unto life eternal.

The Sacramental System rests, as we believe, on a basis in the natural world; to nature, then, may we look, on nature may we freely draw, for a supply of whatever is necessary to convey to us, through the senses, a due apprehension of the meaning and value of that system. Therefore it seems to be of the perpetual fitness of things that Religion should be symbolical in form; that it should wear a striking and appropriate garb, visible to the eye, and expressive of the spirit within. Such is indeed the fact, in the case of every religion which has proved its right to the name by the effects produced on its adherents; and the Catholic Religion is the most convincing and attractive instance of the general law. To the solemn and beautiful Ritual of the Church of Christ your thoughts shall now be directed; and under that term is included everything, small or great, employed by way of rite, ceremony, or symbol, to present to mankind the truth revealed by the Father of the universe and the Ruler of their life. How vast is this subject and how refreshing to one who is tired of the noise of the world and the strife of tongues! How satisfying to the soul which loves the good, the beautiful, and the true! Think of the worship of the Church; how deep the impress it has stamped upon the world; how often of old it subdued the wild barbarian by its awe and reverence; how it has melted the hearts of those who beheld it for the first time, or, after long absence, saw the solemn pageantry again; how it attracts and satisfies the devout, transforms the fierce and cruel, converts the sinner, and seems to open to the toilers in this world's night a gate into heaven. It is wonderful to note how the Church, with her ancient Creed and her equally ancient liturgical Use—in essentials the same all the world through—has held her place, surviving every empire of the earth, outliving assaults, falsifying each prediction of failure, and chanting her "*De Profundis*" over the graves of the enemies by whom she has been assailed from generation to generation! Nay, even when, under pressure and perhaps inadvertently, men have rejected and flung away their birthright in that grand traditional system of faith and worship, we fail not to find them growing more and more restless and uneasy, while trying to recover, if not the substance, at least the shadow of what once was theirs. It is, indeed, a touching sight to behold the children whose fathers repudiated the old and venerable forms of Christian worship, now groping their way back to the place of parting, to see if anything, and if so, what, could be recovered where so much was thrown away. What a wonderful story is told, by comparing the New England meeting-house of two hundred and fifty years ago—that depressing, barn-like structure, four-square, painted white, and having no semblance of a house of God—with one of those magnificent edifices, built in correct ecclesiastical style and externally faultless, in which the descendants of the ancient Puritans now assemble for their Sunday devotions! The principle on which symbolical and liturgical religion rests is deeply rooted in human nature; it is an instinct, a demand, implying universal need. The science of Christian Liturgics, based on those needs of mankind, stands eminent among all sciences; rich in material, congenial, attractive, satisfying. In Christianity, when sincerely and simply taught, will inevitably be found that quality referred to by John Mason Neale, in his preface to his translation of Durandus, which he calls SACRAMENTALITY. Types of Christianity occur, no doubt, in which this element seems wanting; but are they not corruptions of our religion? may they not be described as cases of emasculated or desiccated Christianity? True Christianity cannot be false to the general postulate on which religion is built; to the nature of man, to the design of God in making us what we are, to the drift of history from the beginning of the world to this day. The Sacramental System can be traced in the heavens above and in the earth beneath, in the Incarnate Word, and in ourselves; the science of Christian symbolism is its inseparable attendant; from pole to pole, and from the one sea to the other, it proclaims the unity of the works of God in nature and in grace.

By an ineradicable instinct, by a sense of fitness, and by a sensible need, men seek and find—whatever their religion—some means of giving outward expression to their faith. Let them believe what they will, be it right or wrong, false or true, they must announce it in visible sign or act. The more they believe, the more free will be their use of ritual and symbolical helps; the purer their faith, the more noble and affecting its expression. Conversely, as men lose their hold on a world beyond this, believing less and less, the more dry and dull must their worship become, till, when they reach the end, and believe nothing, acts of worship cease, because the motive to worship exists no more. I repeat it: all nations, people, and languages, without exception, so far as they have had any religion, have felt the need of means to convey religious ideas to themselves and to others. God, in choosing a people as His own, and making them His agents in keeping the light aflame in the darkness of the earth, instituted a full, minute, and splendid ritual system as an adjunct to that work. The Holy Church throughout the world, heir of the elder branch of the family, followed the indication of the Divine Will. For the "Origines Liturgicæ" we go back to those days when the worship of the synagogue expanded into that of the Christian assemblies. What we now possess and enjoy may be traced to norms in the sub-apostolic age. The utmost importance attaches to these things; they make for help and encouragement, for accuracy in teaching, for precision in thought, for conservation of dogma, for edification of believers, for signs to faith, for reminders of duty, for object lessons in divine knowledge, for comfort and consolation in a world of care. Even the conflicts which have raged from time to time, and often with mob-fury and frenzy of fanatics, about the Ritual Question, attest its importance in the eye of mankind. We may count on a general consent to the proposition that Symbolism is valuable only for what it expresses, and that a ritual which means nothing is not worth keeping up. The men who built and decorated the great cathedrals, and developed in them the full glory of worship, did so, not for amusement or for the gratification of a dry and selfish æstheticism, but under an impulse which compelled them to make their loyalty and devotion known to the world, and to give due expression to the truths to which they were devoted, heart and soul; while, on the other hand, they who, roaring in the midst of the congregations, set fire to the holy places, brake down the carved work thereof with axes and hammers, and defiled the dwelling-place of God's Name, did so under the impression that they were doing Him service as reformers of abuses and exterminators of falsehood and error. On each side, by friend and foe alike, is witness borne to the power of ritual and its influence on the people.*

Let us think of this matter, first, from what may be termed an *à priori* point of view, and then in some of its historical and practical aspects.

Two things seem so clear that they need no argument to prove their truth; it is impossible to state the articles of any religion without the use of dogmatic terms; it is next to impossible to keep a system of doctrine intact without the help of symbols apt to represent and teach it.

"As thought cannot be expressed without language, or some outward sign and representation, either in science or religion, so it is an absolute necessity to employ signs, words, or symbols, to embody and teach the facts of both If the

---

* Even Auguste Comte, having swept away the Christian religion, and substituted for it his system of philosophy, was fain to invent and contrive a religion and a ritual to match his new discoveries; he has his church, his hierarchy, and his pontiff, his mimicry of ecclesiastical rites and institutions, and his travesty of the Christian sacraments We also learn that the recent school of sceptics, who march under the name and invocation of "Robert Elsmere," have set up a church in London, wherein they carry on some kind of worship, the Lord knows what, after their own peculiar ideas So even the most extreme among the enemies of the Faith attest the power of the principle which underlies our ritual and liturgical service of the True God

mathematician cannot do without his signs and formulæ, or the merchant without his figures and secret marks, so the religion of all antiquity could not do without its symbols And it is difficult to know how any religion can be preserved in its purity and integrity without symbols or exact and uniform expressions of truth, from which there shall be no variation. It is possible that, in the lapse of time, with the increase of wealth and luxury and the usual degeneracy of morals and decay of pure religion consequent upon such a state of things, the first symbols of a people might come to lose their significance or influence, and others of a more debased character be added to the list And it is further possible that all symbols might be taken for the things or gods which they represented, at least among the ignorant and depraved, and among all such as were incapable of abstract thought, or were more under the influences of the senses than of faith or reason But how to have a religion and worship for a people at large, without some kind of external form and expression, or how to preserve and transmit such religion and worship without symbols and records, it is next to impossible to say " *

The use of Symbolism is coeval with the human race; it is a result of the constitution of man's nature; the desire, the need, are implanted in the heart from the very beginning.† Divine truth is presented to man as a whole, and not to one depart-

---

* "Monumental Christianity, or the Art and Symbolism of the Primitive Church as Witnesses and Teachers of the One Catholic Faith and Practice " By John P Lundy, p. 4

† See C O. Muller, quoted by Dr. Lundy, pp 23, 24

ment or function of his nature only; it has to do with us as we are, complete in body, soul, and spirit; every part is concerned in and affected by what God makes known. And therefore, unless religion has a visible, audible, palpable side, it cannot meet the entire man, much less the whole human brotherhood. Men need no commandment on that point; nature tells them what must be done; and just as soon as they perceive the existence of an object of worship, they seek and find a symbolical method of rendering homage; some sign, some form, is instantly appropriated to that purpose. On the instincts of humanity, on needs universally felt and admitted, rests the Liturgical system of the Church; nay, it is thus also with every system of worship at any time or in any place used among men.

But symbolism is not only indispensable to the expression of the faith, it is equally necessary to its preservation. Our thoughts are unstable and changeful; they are not an unerring guide; left to ourselves, without safeguard or check, we cannot be trusted from day to day; "the Lord knoweth the thoughts of man that they are vain." * To steady

---

* Ps xciv. 11

them, we need visibles which endure. It would be tiresome to quote the "*segnius irritant*" of the bard of the Sabine farm; you know the lines, perhaps, by heart; and you know that the words are true. The value of Ritual consists in its aptness to teach, and its ability to preserve and transmit what it teaches. A ritual which means nothing is an anomaly, the melancholy shadow of something dead and gone. A meagre and defective ritual is helpless to prevent variation in doctrine. Truth may be held for a while, without this aid to our weakness, but not for long. Men of powerful intellect and strong convictions have now and then declined the help of rite and symbol, and set at naught whatever makes for exterior reverence and beauty in religion; but their temporary success was due to the movement of the tide of controversy; as the combative spirit lost power, and quietness and calm returned, disintegration in thought and belief followed. Reformers, inspired by a supreme conviction of the truth of some pet tenet, or a sense of responsibility and importance as guardians of a favorite line of doctrine, may go on for a time without the aid of those adjuncts which in general are necessary for the defence and maintenance of religion; but when the early zeal dies out, with the impulse which it gave, the descent into indifference is accelerated by the removal of the brakes from the wheel. And so with the Catholic Religion. While in its ritual and symbolism there is no value whatever apart from the truths which they enshrine and disclose in their characteristic way, it is impossible to see how that religion could be kept up in the world without their help; as matter of experience, it 'has not been kept up where the old and suitable forms and rites have been discarded. The Symbol, devoutly and intelligently used, becomes an agent in strengthening our intellectual apprehension. Attitudes expressive of awe and reverence develop those feelings, and become secondary causes thereof. Many persons say: "I make this sign, I use that ceremony, because I need them; if I did not, I might lose my faith." And they are right in their statement of the case; for we are imitative beings; we are helped by what we see; under the law of association, conduct and opinion are invariably influenced by acts, sights, sounds, subjected to the senses, and carrying an impression to the mind and heart. Many have owed their conversion to the eye and the ear, engaged by some symbolical presentment of a vital truth, who would have been deaf to the most forcible appeal to the logical faculty; and this because they were men; not spirit and mind only, but body and senses also; and because idealism was not adequate to their need. How solemnly and earnestly is the case presented by the apostle in describing how the human race was brought to the right knowledge of God Himself! "That which was from the beginning, which we have heard, which we have seen with our eyes, which we have looked upon, and our hands have handled, of the Word of Life, that declare we unto you."* God did not reveal Himself to abstract thought; nor is the knowledge of Him and our relation to Him derivable from abstract thought. He came among us, and was seen and heard in the visible form of that human nature in which He dwelt; now we still see Him, in the religion of Sacramentality and Symbolism, which do for us what sight and touch and hearing did for those who were near Him in the days of His flesh.

In accordance with these principles, the Catholic Church has presented, and still presents, the truth, through her solemn and beautiful ritual, to mankind. We believe, we must believe, we cannot but believe, in the truth and reality of what is con-

---

* 1 St. John, 1 1, 2

stantly spoken of as the worship of nature. We
gladly adopt the term, and assign to it a practical
value; not using it as a rhetorical phrase but as the
statement of a fact. The heavens declare the glory
of God.* The stars had a voice in the morning of
the world,† and still the entire firmament speaks
His praise. Nature, through all her realms, knows
how to express the gratitude and joy which come
of existence according to her Creator's will. Could
we but see beneath the surface, we should, no
doubt, find in everything that hath breath a power
to praise the Lord ‡ and a good will thereto; if we
could hear better than we do with these gross ears
of ours, we should, no doubt, receive the harmonies
of a grand anthem of gladness perpetually sung to
God, through kingdom after kingdom of His worlds.
Now the worship of the Catholic Church was meant
to be, and is, a response to this inarticulate and—
to us, but only to us—inaudible action of worship; §
and whatever of breadth, of splendor, of impressive-
ness, of melody are in the Versicle should appear in
the Respond. The worship of nature is like an

---

* Psalm xix 1. † Job, xxxviii 7. ‡ Psalm cl. 6
§ For some very interesting and valuable thoughts and statements
on what has been called superhuman vision and the rhythmical
movement in Nature, see Canon MacColl's "Christianity in Relation to Science and Morals," pp 222–236

Antiphon, given out, full and clear, through earth and sky and sea; and then the psalm is taken up, with that Antiphon for its suggestive inspiration, and it rolls forth from the temples of the Lord, wherein He dwells, and its sound goes out into all lands. Why should not His worship be as rich, as magnificent, as it can be made? Why should there not go into it as much of beauty, majesty, and refined culture as faithful souls and ardent minds and reverent and devoted spirits can contribute for an oblation to the Lord? What else can it be but visible and symbolical? We have seen that the whole system of the created universe is sacramental in its cast; that the sacramental principle is traceable everywhere in nature; that under visible forms spiritual and moral truths are made known to intelligent inhabitants of the world. So the whole material universe becomes tributary to God's Church, the constituted teacher of the nations, the witness and keeper of the truth. Since God has been pleased to appropriate certain elements of this world, and in particular the element of water, the flour of wheat, the juice of the grape, the oil of the olive, and, sanctifying them to spiritual and supernatural uses, has lifted them to an unheard-of honor, is it not meet and right that nature should continue to contribute her choicest treasures for oblation in those places in which her own has thus already been glorified? The rock of the mountain side, the trees of the forest; frond and flower, the glory of Lebanon, the fir tree, the pine tree, and the box together; the gold, the silver, the precious stones; the products of the loom; color, lights, sweet sounds, all kinds of music; nay, everything whereby God can be praised and gratitude can be expressed, and everything apt to carry a meaning or present a truth, is here in place. That is a healthful instinct which bids us make our churches as beautiful as we can and our ritual attractive and impressive. It helps us to realize that God is one in nature and in the Church. It is a fatal error to divorce the worship of God in nature and the worship of God in the Church as if they had nothing in common, for if His worship in our Christian assemblies be allowed to sink into something so cold, so bald, so dull, so lifeless as we often see it, why should not men turn away from that unworthy and unsatisfying routine and get them to the open air, crying: "Give me the light, the color, the music; give me the blue of the sky, the brilliance of the flowers, the softness of the green sward; the reflection of the clouds in lake and stream, the songs and carols of the birds; these lift my soul, these warm my heart, these realize God to me as He never could be realized within four whitewashed walls, in prosy, unreal talk, in discordant droning of unmusical verse; the worship of nature is more true to the ideal than what you ask me to offer in your synagogue or auditorium." Let it ever be in your thoughts, this alliance between the ritual of nature and the ritual of Holy Church. Let us welcome the idea of the offering of her best, by nature, to the promotion of the greater glory of the Lord, and of our duty to accept that gift in good faith. It is of the fitness of things that this should be so; it is the expression of our conviction of the unity of God's works in nature and in grace; it is our protest against the spirit which thinks that we do honor to God by making His worship mean, slovenly, and contemptible. In fact, the whole system of ritual splendor and magnificence lies in germ in the institution of the two sacraments as necessary to salvation. The Church has responded to a suggestion which it was impossible to misunderstand. She has invested the simple act of baptism, the simple acts of breaking bread and blessing a cup, with a rich abundance of symbolical ceremonies, in order to stamp more deeply on the minds of her children the ideas connected with those sacraments, the truths which they enshrine, the benefits which they apply ; she shows forth, by every agency adapted to the purpose, the exalted nature of our first grafting into Christ, the indescribable mystery of growth upward into Him and into eternal life, by feeding on His flesh and blood. These adjuncts are not essential to the validity of the sacraments, but they have a use and a fitness which place them beyond legitimate objection.*

But it is said that these things are for the vulgar only, and that men of a high order of intelligence do not need them. We are not careful to reply to that ancient, ill-tempered slur. What are contemptuously called the vulgar constitute, in point of fact, the great mass of mankind. To the poor the gospel was preached ; " to this man will I look, saith the Lord, even to him that is poor and of a contrite spirit and trembleth at my word." † Religion is for such as these, first of all ; not for a coterie of self-opinionated philosophers, nor for any man, whosoever he be, who walks in pride of intellect or heart ; and against the appeal of the poor in spirit, and the unerring instinct of the mass of man-

---

* See Moehler's " Symbolism," vol 1 p 311
† Isa lxvi 2

kind, rationalistic objections avail not. The rationalist may deny, he cannot affirm; he may pull down, he cannot build up; he never can invent a religion which will meet the want of the race. Our argument against that cold idealism which makes men iconoclasts is justified by common sense, and even more strongly by experience. "To confine religion entirely to spirituals," says an old author, "may perhaps have been the attempt of well-meaning men, but certainly of bad philosophers. They were unacquainted with human nature, and did not foresee that their attempt must terminate in perfect Quietism." As little do they perceive who throw away the Christian ritual and yet hope to keep Christian dogma, that the loss of the former involves the loss of the latter, and that he who discards the sign will ultimately be forced to part with the thing signified.

It was not without the highest authority that the Church of the latter days developed her ritual system. Almighty God was the author of that order which preceded it, and out of which it grew. His directions were comprehensive and minute, and the result was impressive and magnificent. Enough may be gathered from the Holy Scriptures and from external testimony to show that the service of the ancient Church must have been stately and profoundly impressive. To that, as to a norm, they looked, who had the ordering of Christian worship. Their reliance on symbolism, their appreciation of the fine arts in their various branches, are evident from the beginning. The pictures and symbols in the Catacombs, the palm branch, the Agnus Dei, the fish, the cross, are instances of the desire to give visible expression to faith. That Christian worship was, from the first, liturgical will only be denied by those who are influenced by a strong distaste for it. That the Christian converts began to adorn and decorate their places of worship as soon as they were relieved from the fear of persecution, is matter of history. More and more beautiful, more and more rich and splendid became the order of their worship, till it attained a culmination in the ages when the great cathedrals of the world were built. Glorious things, indeed, are spoken of thee, thou city of God!

Take the cathedral idea, as it lived in the mind of the men of old and was partially realized by their hands, and consider if anything be lacking to make it the most splendid conception of holy symbolism. Let us imagine ourselves before one of those superb objects which constitute the admiration and the despair of our colder and less religious day. Here stands the sacred pile, every square foot teaching a lesson and expressing a truth; addressing intellect, heart, and senses together; showing man the glory of God, the mystery of his own being, the wonders of time and eternity. The western front faces a storm-swept world, as a barrier of rock the angry sea; figures of Archangel and Angel, Apostles, Saints, and Warriors seem to repel the powers of darkness, grotesque shapes here and there suggest the strange, incongruous elements so warded off lest they might disturb the peace of the Holy City. The western towers represent the Apostolic Ministry, firm and unshaken. The portals, enriched with leaf, flower, and fruit, and deeply cusped and shafted, welcome the approaching pilgrim, whom sweet and peaceful countenances also regard as he draws nigh. He sees the long sweep of the wall and roof line, the transepts, the flying buttresses, throwing their arms across the sky; and there, above, the spire rises, and melts away into the air, catching the first rays of the morning light, flushed by the sunset, and holding up the everlasting cross amidst the stars of night. Enter, and hushed now be soul and heart, for we are in another world. Who does not know the impression produced on first standing inside the great cathedral doors? There are the calm of the deep green woods, the "stillness of the central sea " The arcades of the forest are before us; piers and columns stand to the right and left, like the monarchs of the grove, above is the roof for a sky; pictures, mosaics, colors, rainbow hues, make it "all glorious within." And then, the holy of holies beyond!

> "Such trembling joy the soul o'erawes,
>   As nearer to Thy shrine she draws
>   And now before the choir we pause.
>
> "From each carved nook and fretted bend,
>   Cornice and gallery seem to send
>   Tones that with seraph hymns might blend.
>
> "Three solemn parts together twine
>   In harmony's mysterious line,
>   Three solemn aisles approach the shrine " *

Lesser altars, each with its ornaments, catch the eye, but it rests, finally, upon the central throne of the Presence of our Lord. And now, it may be, while eyes are full, and heart as though it could hold no more, shall come the sound of music, which, rolling in deep diapason, fills the air; and chants are heard like the voices of eternity and the songs of the

---
* "Christian Year " Trinity Sunday

New Jerusalem; and forth, in procession, with cross and banner, with cope and shining vestment, come figures, which approach, and ascend the grades of the choir and the altar steps, and show forth The Death, till He come, and make solemn memorial of His Passion, interceding for the sins of the world, praying for "the whole state of Christ's Church militant." This is the culmination, the triumph of Sacramentality and Symbolism; true to our nature; perfectly adapted to the law of our constitution; precious, not in itself nor for itself alone, but for the things which it teaches and for those spiritual realities which it thus presents to the understanding and the faith.

Bryant, in his "Thanatopsis," represents the universe as ministering to man in his death:

> "The hills,
> Rock-ribbed and ancient as the sun—the vales
> Stretching in pensive quietness between;
> The venerable woods, rivers that move
> In majesty, and the complaining brooks
> That make the meadows green, and poured round all
> Old ocean's gray and melancholy waste,
> Are but the solemn decorations all
> Of the great tomb of man."

The thought of the poet, exquisitely though it be

disclosed, is depressing. There is another side to this; we may think of nature in another way; we may realize her as ministering to us in our life, as coming to us in shining garments rather than in mourning weeds; as chanting meanwhile a "Sursum Corda" rather than a "Requiem Æternam." Life, not death, is the message of the Gospel; beauty, not ugliness, the vesture of the King's Daughter; light, not darkness, the boon of nature to believing souls; and the rays derived from her mysterious shrine may better be used to kindle the sanctuary lamp before the altar, than to touch to flame the candles which flicker beside the trestles of the dead.

When, under some sinister influence or some wrong guidance, men, rejecting all this glory and beauty, turn away to their own devices, they leave things which belong to their peace. They go into a chilly air, they begin a long descent; they lose, in losing the sign, those things which it signifies, the help which the symbol was intended to give. Less and less shall they know about worship; more and more hard and intellectual shall become their religion; the sanctities of the altar service shall be replaced by the attraction of listening to a set discourse; the gratification of the ear, the exercise of the critical faculty on some favorite orator's eloquent efforts, shall become the prominent motives to draw them to the place of meeting. Slowly, and step by step, come changes in this declining progress; men bow no longer at the Sacred Name; they kneel no longer; they sit, to praise, to pray; the more bare the edifice, the better it seems to its purpose; there is no font, no altar, no organ, there is no belief in regeneration or the real presence; there is no priesthood; there is no garb for officiant; there is no authority but that of private judgment and individual taste. So proceeds the evolution; and still, beyond, to more barren forms, when we come to the frigid silence of Quietists, who sit waiting for the Spirit to move them, and discard every external in religion. There is no farther step, save that of imperturbable agnosticism; which, when we reach, we are at the frigid pole, where the Solemn Ritual of the Catholic Church is replaced by an inarticulate cry addressed, none knows to what. True to theory and close to fact is the picture drawn by Mr. Mallock, of the logical end of the rejection of the symbolism of the sacramental Church. Paul will instruct Virginia in the solemn and unspeakably significant worship of the Positivism, which admits no God, no soul, no supernatural order, and, above all, no hell. He will show her

OUTWARD GLORY AND INWARD GRACE. 205

what true religion and true worship are; he has an audible and a reasonable liturgy which gives utterance to the religion of exact thought.

"'Let us both join our voices,' he says, 'and let us croon at the moon.' The professor at once began a long, low howling. Virginia joined him until she was out of breath

"'Oh, Paul,' she said at last, 'is this more rational than the Lord's Prayer?'

"'Yes,' said the professor, 'for we can analyze and comprehend that, but true religious feeling, as Professor Tyndall tells us, we can neither analyze nor comprehend See how big nature is, and how little—ah, how little!—we know about it Is it not solemn, and sublime, and awful? Come, let us howl again'

"The professor's devotional fervor grew every moment At last he put his hand to his mouth, and began hooting like an owl, till it seemed that all the island echoed to him" *

" HE GAVE THEM THEIR DESIRE, AND SENT LEANNESS WITHAL INTO THEIR SOUL."

We have long since passed the point at which the return to the old ways in our branch of the Church excited anger and provoked to iconoclastic rioting. The Oxford Movement began by the

---

* " The New Paul and Virginia, or Positivism on an Island," by W. H Mallock, pp 124-129

recovery of doctrine and dogma, obscured and all but lost in the age of latitudinarian and Protestant error; the ritual revival followed as its legitimate fruit. In some points it is open to criticism; we may regret, perhaps deplore, the line taken in the development in certain directions; but whatever mistakes have been made, the general course has been right and true. John Mason Neale's prediction, in his spirit-stirring lines, "The Good Old Times of England," has been fulfilled to the letter,* and each day widens the range of that victorious progress. Meanwhile, the work within our own borders has the sympathy and approval of multitudes of friends and lovers of God, in other folds than ours, who are following as fast as could be expected in the path on which we are pioneers. And often, watching these things, do men bow the head, and give God thanks for the day when the beauty and the glory are thus coming back, as if they could hear, in the air about them, the cadence of the prophet's words:

"Et aedificabunt deserta a seculo et ruinas antiquas erigent, et instaurabunt civitates desertas, dissipatas in generationem et generationem " †

---

* "Hierologus," ch IV. pp 101-103   † Isa lxi. 4.

Only let this be said by way of cautel. What we most need, everywhere, to-day, is reality in religion, and yet, so strangely is temptation fitted to human weakness, that without suspecting it we may be powerfully drawn to unreality and untruth, like those who pursue a phantom and grasp at a shadow. It is a distinct temptation to have and to use things, without attaching a meaning to them; to retain creeds, and yet to put on the words whatever sense we please; to have forms, but to disclaim what they naturally convey to the eye and the ear; to use a ritual, but at the same time to say that it is without doctrinal signification. That is the instant danger of the hour; against that we must be ever on the watch; it is Satan's masterpiece to take what ought to make for stronger faith, deeper reverence, and more sensible apprehension of things unseen and invisible, and, having extracted the kernel and marrow, to leave us an empty shell, a worthless husk. Unreality in religion makes unreality in the daily life; God forbid that we be involved in the downfall to which it leads! God forbid that any one of us be found saying, or saying Amen to, prayers with which the conscience does not go along; reciting the Creed, yet inwardly muttering, "I do not really mean it;" making vows of obedience and conformity, with a mental reservation; bowing the knee in the house of God, yet saying secretly, "I do not believe in this," or "I do this only because I find it becoming, attractive, æsthetic." Better no religion than one which amounts to no more than a hollow form, a piece of decorative art, a cerement wrapped around the bones of a dead faith. Better no vows, than vows which a man intends to keep only so long as his views remain the same; better no plight of troth in marriage than one which is to stand good only till some new love supplants the old; better no words than words twisted into a falsehood and a lie; better no rites than rites which mean nothing.

And this leads me to my last word on the subject which has so long engaged our thoughts: the Sacramental System finds its inward manifestation in the life of the soul. Here we pass from symbols to what they signify, from the visible to the invisible; we enter a region of tender, shadowed, solemn thoughts, of personal experiences, of contacts with the spiritual world, where one walks trembling yet joyful in the presence of the Holy Ghost.

For it is the Spirit of God, the Lord and Life Giver, who acts on us through externals, to renew and restore the Divine Image within us and to make us meet to be partakers of the inheritance of the saints. We hear of Christ so constantly, He is so perpetually talked about, that it reminds us of His own prediction · "They shall say, Lo, here is Christ; or, Lo, He is there; behold, He is in the deserts, or He is in the secret places." * There be false Christs, and false prophets; almost as many Christs as there are persons who prate of Him and pretend to have fathomed the mystery of His being, His person, and His acts. But still, Christ is all in all; and to live His life and to have His image reflected in the heart is the conclusion of the whole matter. For the knowledge of our Lord we must trust to close study of such representation of Him as we have; His portrait is painted for us in many a psalm of the Old Testament, in many a prophecy; in His own Beatitudes, in words of Evangelist and Apostle; it is a picture of One who is with God, and in God, truly man also, humble, lowly, long-suffering, meek; poor in spirit, never doubting, never disputatious; leading a life divine, yet folded around in human garb, in perfect sympathy with everything that lives; known to the spirits of the lost, fenced around by legions of

---

* St Matt. xxiv 23, 26.

angels, familiar with the marvels of the invisible realm. It must be pronounced impossible to reproduce even any faint likeness of this consummate life, this superhuman character, unless the spirit of self-trust and self-will be laid aside; unless a man be clothed on with deep humility; unless he be imbued with ideas and impressions derived from faith in the invisible; unless he desires that which God doth promise; unless the saints and the angels and the spiritual world are as real to him as the tenants of the world in which we now live. It cannot be demanded of the rationalist, the agnostic, the sceptic, that they should turn out of their workshop an image absolutely foreign to their conception of what man should be. An invincible faith in things unseen; a realization of the supernatural realm with its marvellous contents; a constant tending towards God, in holding out the hand for Him, feeling after Him, seeking to be where He is, sure of nothing where He is not discerned, these are the factors of the re-creation in Christ, and these are in vital harmony and accord with the system displayed under holy sacraments and symbols apt to the work of the training of the soul, the renewal of the heart. The Christian dispensation, to judge of it from its description in the Holy

Gospels and the New Testament writings, was intended to do a specific work among us. It was designed to act on the heart, to form a peculiar character, and to develop certain tendencies in man; to convince him of his own littleness and of the greatness of God; to bring him to God in perfect self-renunciation, and to make him very calm and strong in a strength not his by nature, nor in any way his own. The result, where the system has its way untrammelled, is that, to the disciple so instructed, the whole world becomes instinct with solemn mysteries and full of things divine; life is, in its experiences, a continual lesson in the dealings of our merciful Lord with us; things about us are more than they seem to be; visible objects stand for invisibles; there are meanings in every department of nature which the natural eye cannot take in; dreams, signs, visions, omens are not to be despised; stars and flowers and mountains, rivers, lakes, the ancient hills, the wide and wandering sea, all have, in truth and reality, a voice for the soul; the year has its divisions, the day its hours, through which the mystery of redemption is continually repeated; every duty rests on a law of the God of righteousness, every action should be done to His glory, every work begun, continued, and ended in Him. Under this tuition men acquire a readiness to admit the inexplicable, to credit the improbable, to believe—as St. Augustine expressed it in his noted paradox—the impossible. They are not confined within the bound of flesh and sense; they do not starve on the thin scrannel straw of Positivism; they are prepared for things most marvellous, most unaccountable; they apprehend an unfathomable mystery in their own life; they walk ringed about with mystery—not such mystery as leads to helpless, abject surrender of intellectual effort to sound it, but a mystery to which they know they have a key: everything that occurs has its meaning; everything works together for their good; the *beyond* is far more real than the *present;* the Bible is a wonder book in which every recorded miracle is gladly accepted; prayer has its answer; God is present; in the holy places He meets them and they are with Him; angels and ministers of grace surround them; departed souls commune with them; all live to God. They know that the human body is the temple of the Holy Ghost; that it contains a germ of the spiritual body that is to be; they know that the whole creation is interested in the destiny of man and is looking for the adoption, the redemption, of the body. Such are the convictions of the men of faith, and how can they be strengthened and confirmed so surely as under that system of which we have been meditating in these Lenten studies? Where faith is at a minimum, and reverence for the supernatural is deemed superstition, it must be impossible to develop such a character and spirit as have been now hurriedly sketched. Where it exists it will stamp its special mark on the form, the manner, and the features, according to the sincerity of its reception and the completeness of its rule. To what extent soever the Catholic religion acts upon us, to that extent it must transform us; if there be much of our own native infirmity and imperfection, its influence will be apparently diminished; if we give ourselves up to it without reserve and without fear, men will perceive the fact and confess that the unseen powers are with us of a truth; if we have made slow and very little progress here, we shall have the more to learn in that future state where our education is to be continued; if we have advanced rapidly in this lower school, the entrance shall be abundant into the courts above. The visible impress of holiness is the presage of immortality, the sign of the life with Christ in God, the assurance of a resurrection in the new and glorious body which is to be man's heavenly dress. More of these things shall we know as faith comes back; that faith which is the substance of our dreams, the evidence of the truth of our convictions; which is an anchor of the soul thrown into that within the veil and holding us fast to our moorings; which leads men to renounce the world, to despise its promises and defy its power, to seek those things which are above, where Christ sitteth at the right hand of God. Come, Holy Ghost, and lift the covering spread on the face of unbelief and lead us safely to those blessed seats, where we shall see face to face; where the signs and symbols now used shall be exchanged for the substance and reality, wherein shall be no further change forever and ever.

"AND I SAW NO TEMPLE THERE. AND THEY NEED NO CANDLE, NEITHER LIGHT OF THE SUN; FOR THE LORD GOD GIVETH THEM LIGHT, AND THEY SHALL REIGN FOR EVER AND EVER."

APPENDED NOTES.

APPENDED NOTES.

NOTE I. (See page 24.)

Dr. Pusey has a sermon on the subject of the sympathy of nature with man in his sorrow and pain. (See Parochial Sermons, Vol. II. Sermon XVII., "Groans of Unrenewed and Renewed Nature;" Rom. viii. 22, 23.) The reader may be glad to have the following extract from that wonderful discourse:

"Such, then, is the first sense of this great and mysterious passage, that all nature, having suffered together, shall be restored together. Things animate and inanimate, as being the works of God (as we see in the use of Holy Scripture and even in the very works themselves), bear in themselves some likeness to their Maker, and traces of His hands. Things seen speak of things unseen. How does the bright gladdening glow of light speak of the purity of Light inapproachable, that one may not scan it with too bold a gaze; how it warms, heals, lightens, directs, penetrates, transfigures into itself, gladdens our inmost souls. And yet all around us and in us bear also sad tokens of the fall. As then to us death is to be the gate of immortality and glory, so in some way to them. Whence Holy Scripture says elsewhere, 'the earth shall wax old like a garment, and they that dwell therein shall die in like manner.' We are to die 'in like manner' with the earth. As then we, so many as are in Christ, perish not utterly, but put off only corruption, to be, by a new and immortal birth, clothed with incorruption, so also they

"Again, as Holy Scripture says of us, 'the dead shall be raised incorruptible, and we shall be *changed*,' so, in their measure, of them, 'as a vesture shalt Thou change them, and they shall be changed.' It says not only 'shall perish,' but be 'changed,' and renewed to good. 'The heavens being on fire shall be dissolved, and the elements shall melt with fervent heat.' Yet the fire which burns up heaven and earth shall but free them from the wrongs which they endure at our hands, the bondage in which they have been held to corruption and vanity, and, cleansing them from the stains and defilements of our sins, shall yield them pure, 'a new heaven and a new earth,' new for us renewed, incorrupt for us undefiled; so that as our dwelling-place has, as yet, been marred by our sin, then should the love of God for us overflow upon it, and the glory of His presence, which shall be our joy, shall array it too with a glad brightness, in harmonious sympathy with our joy. 'As our human body shall be endued with a certain supernatural form of glory, so the whole creation of sense, in that glory of the sons of God, shall obtain a newness of glory, and the former things passing away, and the oldness of decay, He shall make all things new.'

"Elsewhere, too, Holy Scripture lends a voice to mute and inanimate nature, saying, 'All the trees of the wood shall rejoice before the Lord, for He cometh, He cometh to judge the earth.' 'Break forth into singing, ye mountains, O forest and every tree therein.' Wherein it speaks doubtless in part in a spiritual sense, how *they* shall abound and overflow with joy in God, whom He hath planted in His courts, filled with the life-giving, ever-flowing sap of His Spirit, and made fruit-bearing trees; or those again, eminent in light and holiness, who, like mountains, are rooted deep in humility, pierce the clouds through faith, and catch the first beams of the Sun of Righteousness. But it seems to picture too how heaven and earth shall, when He cometh, wear a dress of joy.

So the prophet says again that our earth shall glow with a fuller light from heaven, in that 'the light of the moon shall be as the light of the sun, and the light of the sun sevenfold, as the light of seven days.'

"Such glorious tokens of our immortal state, such wonderful signs of oneness and love, such touching lessons of our passing away and our abiding, does God shed all around us, that the very creation which we misuse should mind us of our end, earth, sea, and sky should bid us love not them, but Him who made them, should by its very state and being, its beauty and decay, tell us to long for Him for whom itself seemeth to yearn, the perfection of beauty, infinite in perfection, who alone abideth forever

"Yet since Holy Scripture saith 'the *whole* creation groaneth and travaileth in birth-pain together with' us, it, in some sense, includes all created being, and tells us that all, from highest to lowest, have an interest in our redemption, all are made subject, as it were, to some imperfection, all, with long and longing expectations, look 'for the revelation of the sons of God,' when our life, now 'hidden with Christ in God,' shall be disclosed, when 'Christ, who is our life, appearing, we also shall appear with Him in glory'"

My dear friend, William Fitzhugh Whitehouse, Esq., now and for some two years past in England, has recently published a monograph, entitled, "The Redemption of the Body, being an Examination of Rom. viii. 18–23." (London, Elliot Stock, 62 Paternoster Row, E C., 1892.) It is well worth reading, and shows research and close thought. The author will not, I am sure, take exception, if I speak of his work as a " private interpretation " (*ἰδία ἐπίλυσις*), considering that he not only admits but calls attention to the fact that his rendering of the passage is "virtually new." Mr. Whitehouse's contention is, that the word translated "creature" or "creation" signifies the human body. He has not succeeded in persuading me to alter my views as to the meaning of St. Paul; but I commend his book to the student, and consider that we have reason to be thankful when we find laymen interesting themselves in theological questions so intelligently as he has done, and treating those questions in so reverent a spirit and with so true an estimate of their importance. Mr. Whitehouse promises us a new and greatly enlarged edition of his work.

NOTE II (See page 74.)

I cannot do justice to the words referred to without quoting the whole passage in which they occur; and I do so the more willingly, because it is well for some of us to see precisely how things strike our brethren who are looking on from outside, and observing the drift among us. The testimony of Dr. Van Dyke as to the real quality of Zwinglianism is particularly valuable:

"We cannot undertake accurately to define what Zwingle taught in regard to the sacraments, nor to harmonize the conflicting testimony of the learned in regard to it. He does not seem to have been consistent with himself. His ardent mind was better qualified to pull down error than to build up the truth. Admitting all that has been said in explanation and defence of his teaching, it is evident that his doctrine fell far below the standard of the reformed confessions. There is historic justice in applying the name 'Zwinglian' to such statements in regard to the Lord's Supper as the following·

"1 That the bread and the wine of the Holy Communion are nothing but naked and bare signs, and that the ordinance itself is simply a commemoration of Christ's death, a badge of our Christian profession, and a pledge of mutual love among believers

"2. That the Lord's Supper is only a sign and seal of *pre-existing* grace in the communicant, and not a means or instrument by which more grace is bestowed upon those who worthily partake of it

"3 That Christ is present and operative for our salvation in the sacrament only in His divine nature and in the *apprehension* of the believing communicant

"4 That the benefits received by the believer at the Lord's table are nothing more than the sacrificial virtue of the Saviour's death on the cross

"5 That the sacramental feeding of the believing soul on Christ, the eating of His flesh, and the drinking of His blood in the Holy Supper, is identical with any and every exercise of faith in Him, and therefore can be done as well elsewhere as at the Lord's table

"6 That the necessity for the observance of the Lord's Supper is simply a necessity of precept, and not a necessity of means In other words, that we are obliged to keep the feast of the Holy Communion only because Christ has commanded it, and not because we are to expect any *special* benefit from its observance.

"Each of these statements will be fully discussed as we proceed Meantime, we cannot forbear to observe that we reject them not only because of their inconsistency with our doctrinal standards and with the teaching of Scripture, but because of the spirit which pervades them and the underlying assumptions on which they are based Zwinglianism is essentially *rationalistic* in the evil sense of the word. Its chief effort is to explain away or reduce to a minimum the mystery of the Lord's Supper. It assumes that the theory which is most level to our comprehension, which brings the Holy Supper nearest to a common meal where Christians have sweet fellowship together, and makes it agree most with ordinary human experience, is for that reason nearest to the truth We have heard Presbyterian ministers, in administering it, eulogizing the absolute simplicity, not only of its symbols, but of its whole design and efficacy ; comparing it to the monument which recalls the memory of some great man, as though that explained its whole meaning and effect; and dwelling with minute particularity upon Christ's physical sufferings, as though our highest purpose in keeping the feast was to look on a pathetic picture and be moved by it. We grow weary in our reading on the subject of the reiterated assertion that this or that view is incomprehensible, unreasonable, or contrary to common sense, and the more so, because the same writers who use such arguments in regard to the Lord's Supper repudiate and denounce them when they are urged by others against the doctrine of the Trinity, the sovereignty of God, the incarnation, the atonement, the resurrection and exaltation of Christ, the vital union of believers with His glorified Person, and the wonder-working power of His Holy Spirit, all of which revealed mysteries pervade, and are embodied in, the transcendent mystery of the Holy Communion

"Perhaps the ripest and the bitterest fruit of this rationalizing about the Lord's Supper may be found in Dean Stanley's 'Christian Institutions' Adopting the idea of Renan, he makes the 'Last Supper a continuation of those earlier feasts in which Christ had blessed and broken the bread and distributed the fishes on the hills of Galilee' He can see no higher character in the communion of the first and second centuries than in the festive dinner of 'a Greek club, where each brought, as to a common meal, his own contribution in a basket, and each helped himself from a common table.' He identifies the Lord's Supper with the love-feasts of the Early Church He admits, indeed, that it was intended by its Founder to be 'a glorification of the power of memory,' but in his account of what is thus to be remembered he is careful to avoid any reference to Christ's death as the sacrifice for sin, and insists only upon His example and teaching as inculcating human charity. In proportion as the observance of this ordinance enables us 'to move in unison' with the parables of the Prodigal Son, the Good Samaritan, and the Good Shepherd, with the Beatitudes on the Galilean mountains, the resignation in Gethsemane, and the courage on Calvary, he affirms that 'it is a true partaking of what the Gospels intended by the body of Christ' He denies that the Lord's Supper is necessary for these ends, and insists that all who move in unison with these moral precepts and examples, 'whether they be Christian in name or not, whether they have or have not partaken of the sacrament, have thus received Christ, because they have received that which was the essence of Christ—His spirit of mercy and toleration'

"There is nothing new in these sentiments But the strange thing is that a clergyman of high position in the Church of England, one accustomed to the public use of her solemn liturgies, should advocate such opinions, that he should claim for them the authority of 'the clear-headed and intrepid Zwingle,' and attempt to reconcile them with the Articles and Formularies of the Episcopal Church, by the vague assertion that 'since the days of Elizabeth a strong Zwinglian atmosphere has pervaded the original theology of the Church of England, and been its prevailing hue'"

NOTE III (See page 96)

The first edition of the tract referred to was published some twenty-five years ago, under the title,

"A Statement on Confession, made by request in the Church of St. John Baptist, Kidderminster, on Sunday, November 15, 1868, by the Rev. C. N. Gray, Curate." The Rev. Milo Mahan, D.D., sometime Professor of Ecclesiastical History in the General Theological Seminary, and at the time of his death Rector of St. Paul's Church, Baltimore, Md., induced by personal considerations, prepared an Introduction to a proposed reprint of this tract, only a few months before his departure out of this world. It was an abridgment of a much longer document, written by him under peculiarly trying circumstances while in the seminary. I have, perhaps, the only existing copy, and it is possible that some day, when the recollection of an old and bitter controversy has died out, that very brilliant and telling production may see the light. What we have of it is so clear, so pungent, and so full of common sense, that I take occasion to reprint it here in full.

"INTRODUCTION

TO THE AMERICAN EDITION OF THE REV. C. N. GRAY'S TRACT, ENTITLED,

'A STATEMENT ON CONFESSION'

"CONFESSION to God is a necessary and commanded act, which, if done at all, should be thoroughly and well done, with every proper help and appliance. Confession to man is not so necessary, nor so commanded. Its advantage arises chiefly from human ignorance and weakness, a proper sense of which will lead every sober person to get counsel and comfort from those who are best qualified to give it For the maxim, 'Confess your sins one to another, and pray one for another,' does not imply promiscuous confession It is enough to confess to such as we can best confide in, conforming to the rules of propriety and order The same principle that leads one to a physician for confession of bodily ailments, or to a lawyer for counsel in troubles of estate, will naturally designate a clergyman for relief in spiritual affairs This is a matter of common sense, conceded by all The reason why it is not more generally acted upon by Protestants is, the dread of Rome Where Satan cannot lead men into evil by love of a false system, he deters them from good by an unreasonable dread An abuse which ceases to be an attraction is converted into a scarecrow.

"In this way it happens that the pastoral office, instead of being an easy and familiar help to our communicants and young people, is becoming more and more an object of dread or suspicion When the staff of the Lawgiver was thrown upon the ground, it became a serpent, when his hand was thrust into his bosom, it was covered with leprosy. Such is the fate now threatening the pastoral office in the Church Our older people, sinking under weights which they are exhorted to lay aside, but with no hand helping them so to do, are less and less intimate with their spiritual guides; our younger people fall insensibly, often through ignorance, into besetting sins, of which no man gives them fair warning. Young and old alike are afraid to see their pastors, except in 'classes'

"Diffident about recommending to others what I know to have been good for myself, I have yet, in cases not a few, here and there felt obliged to do for others what others have done for me. And in the more perilous matter of half-confidences and consultations about private affairs, where the clergy are frequently called to share the secret burden of their brethren, I deem it always an advantage to all parties if the thing can be so religiously conducted as to give the priest the benefit of the CXIIIth Canon of the Church of England, by putting everything confided to him under the seal of the confessional. For, after all, whether we desire it or not, the clergy become the repositories of many secrets. The only difference made by a formal opening of one's grief is, that the spiritual adviser is less tempted to blab or gossip; and cases which I have known to occur, where eloquent ecclesiastics, in the mere heat of speaking, have divulged to the public things manifestly spoken in confidence, could never happen if the clergy were more trusted in a religious way.

"It is true, in a certain degree, that clergymen of all denominations are already very much trusted; and that, going about a good deal from house to house, and hearing a great deal of confidential talk, they become the depositories of all sorts of secrets, the sharers of all sorts of private burdens, the keepers, as it were, of all skeletons in all closets, without putting themselves under the seal of religious silence, and without securing very much opportunity for religious counsel or comfort. But this is often an evil rather than a benefit. There is an immense waste of time, in the first place. There is danger of abuse, in the second place. One satisfactory visit to a parishioner is gotten at the cost of a dozen mere 'calls.' Half-confidences, gossip, tattle, controversy, and the like, take the place of the opening of one's griefs. Moreover, the thing engenders among the clergy that worst disease in a spiritual or a professional man—looseness of tongue. What men receive in mere gossip they are tempted to retail as such. What is uttered in real confidence, with a formal and strict understanding, and only for a religious profit, is buried and put away, as though it had never been uttered. A physician seldom blabs the infirmities of his patients. A lawyer can be as still as the grave where the secrets of a client are involved.

Professional confidence, in fact, is protected by all laws, human and divine

"I have always, therefore, regarded it as a great advantage that when a person wishes to 'see a minister'—that is, when he really wishes to confer with him privately about the state of his soul—there should be, first, perfect freedom so to do without blame or suspicion; and, in the second place, such directions, safeguards, and helps as the Church of England has provided in the Exhortation to the Holy Communion, as well as in other places referred to in the following tract of Mr Gray A pastor's office, like that of a physician, is necessarily a sort of 'confessional,' though we may scruple to call it by that name While we shrink from the evils that long abuse has associated with the Roman doctrine of confession, it would be mere cowardice and folly to confound the abuse with the use

"Many are averse, except in very peculiar cases, to overfrequent confession I have the same feeling To the soul, as to the body, food is better than physic; and beyond a certain point, exercise and rest are better than either They also object to what has sometimes been called 'the heresy of *direction*,' namely, the very common practice—*possibly* more common among Romanists than among us—of walking by other people's consciences rather than by one's own I object to the same But, practically, I have little faith in confession as a means of mere influence One may like his physician very well, if he is an agreeable man otherwise But I doubt whether any one attaches his patients to him, or moulds their politics or religion by the mere goodness of his medicines.

"But however this may be, I have never taught or practised any doctrine of confession without carefully guarding against the notion of *compulsion*, in the first place, which is the *gist* of the Roman doctrine; or of over-frequency, direction, probable opinions, penances in place of conversion, privity to crimes intended or perpetrated, and many other abuses warranted by Roman authority, which I have carefully studied from my youth Nay, in dealing with persons who are disposed to attribute too much to confession, as is often the case both with penitents and with loose men of the world, I have habitually underrated its importance, by showing how easily, like other medicines, it loses its effects In all my innumerable answers on confession, on which I have been appealed to by all sorts of men, and for all sorts of purposes, I have invariably taught, *first of all*, that *confession* should always be *voluntary and unforced*, I might almost say that I *hate* enforced confession, believing it to be destructive of the chief good of confession. I am also averse, except in very peculiar cases, to frequent confessions, believing that over-frequency in the use of such medicine is deleterious ; that for the soul, as for the body, food is better than medicine, and exercise and rest sometimes better than both I have also invariably taught that the Jesuit doctrine of 'probable opinions,' so-called, is immoral ; that no amount of 'penance' is a substitute for conversion ; that 'absolution,' without due promise of amendment, is sacrilegious ; that immodest and over-minute questions or suggestions tend only to evil ; that the habit of confessing only to priests personally unknown, is pride assuming the garb of humility ; that sin alone is the subject of confession, and holiness of life alone a matter of counsel or direction ; that conscience is to be enlightened, not forced ; that while 'the seal of the confessional' is inviolable in legitimate matters of confession, yet to appeal to it, as in the infamous Gunpowder Plot, for meditated sins or crimes, is an outrage to God and man ; that numbering, or weighing, or curious searching out of sins is an unwise thing, if not positively injurious ; that, in short, the rules laid down in Roman Catholic directions, and practised more or less in Roman confessions, are, for the most part, unwarrantable by Catholic teaching ; and to these, and many like corruptions, the loose morals of the Roman Catholic countries may be fairly attributed. These, and similar points, mark out a clear line between confession, popularly so-called, and a proper pastoral care, or, in other words, between the Roman and the Catholic confession.

"Yet I never refuse a sinner the privilege of opening his grief to his pastor, or withhold from him any counsel or comfort I am able to give. I repel no one who comes to me as the Exhortation in the Communion Office directs him. Moreover, I am willing to confess before God and man that the few opportunities I have had of ministering in this way to weak or wounded souls have been, in my judgment, the most fruitful, nay, perhaps the only fruitful, parts of an unworthy ministry, and if I had my life to live over again, I would preach as well as practise it more earnestly than I have done. On the other hand, I am aware that this dealing with men's griefs is a perilous matter, liable to abuses, that Rome especially has caused it to be beset with scandals, that whether in the study, the confessional, the vestry-room, the sick chamber, or in the open church, the intercourse of priest and penitent should be jealously guarded; that every precaution against abuse or calumny which the lawyer may need in his confidential intercourse with his clients, or the physician in his sacred care of his patients, requires to be at least equally observed by those who deal with spiritual troubles; and that consciences had better not be medicined at all, than tampered with by rash or over-timid hands. On this ground, I see much to dislike in the Roman confessional, much to admire in the Greek, which (theoretically) differs little from our own, much to approve in the Anglican, and nothing to desiderate, save only that it should be honestly carried out in the spirit of the Prayer-book. For, as things go now, a man may be easily enough wounded in the house of his friends, and the bruised reeds may be easily broken, but what with our fear of Rome, and our readiness to devour one another—

which is often only another word for our fear of men—the poor, sickly sheep of the flock, if we have any such, are in a sad predicament.

"I do not deny that there is a Catholic doctrine on this subject of confession, and it will give me pleasure to show, presently, how such a doctrine may be ascertained But meanwhile I utterly deny that any such doctrine, however accurately made out, could be any compulsory authority to us. We have the Book of Common Prayer, the Articles, the Homilies, and the like. By them, and them only, can the doctrine of our clergy be tried But so far as our Church is concerned, of which I avow myself a dutiful though unworthy son, or so far as the Catholic Church goes, in which 'I believe'—though I see less of her than my poor heart craves—I find no very 'accurate statement of the doctrine of confession' I find in our admirable formularies, however, a very beautiful exhortation to *confession*, where the sinner thinks he needs it, and to 'counsel, comfort, and absolution,' where the priest is disposed to give it These, with a few other like points here and there, are the 'Catholic doctrine of confession,' so far as I know or teach it in any real sense.

"One may not be able to distinguish, with sufficient accuracy, all points of difference between us and Rome, but it requires very little sense to see that Rome is a great fisher of young people; that she knows what food the young appetite craves, and consequently, if she baits the hook chiefly 'with the benefits of confession,' it is because she knows this to be a most attractive part of her system I have had some experience of what are called 'tendencies to Rome,' and I believe, as the upshot of my experience, that, with young people especially, the desire to go to Rome is, in nine cases out of ten, simply the desire of confession I do not hesitate, therefore, to commend such confession as our Church allows.

"But while I am unwilling to expose myself to ridicule by pretending to any 'sufficient accuracy,' either in this or in any other point of doctrine, yet I think I know what the 'Catholic doctrine of confession' may be safely affirmed to be, in a general and historical way It is a doctrine of *confession* and *absolution* for the relief of sinners, always the same in substance, but carried out in different ways, at different times, and in different places

"In apostolic times, as we learn from a marked example, it may be briefly summed up as follows A communicant commits a manifest or notorious sin , by the ministry of the Church the sin is brought home to his conscience , by the same ministry, acting in the spirit of love, he is cut off from communion, and moved to *open confession* , by the same ministry he gets *absolution*, after due repentance, and so is finally restored to the communion which his sin had forfeited *

"In the early Catholic Church the process was substantially the same, though perhaps with more of severity and less of love Briefly, the sinner was turned out of the Church, and was kept on a long course of prostration in the dust, with weeping, mourning, fasting, supplication, howling, kissing the feet of the faithful, clutching at the garments of the clergy, with exposure to the weather, and the like,† till, his heart being sufficiently triturated and melted, he was finally allowed to *confess* before the whole congregation, and to receive *absolution*, and so to be restored to his former estate

"This was pretty strict discipline , yet it was not severe enough to satisfy the great party called *Puritans*, who contended that the sinner should be given over to Satan entirely, so far as communion went, and be denied *confession* and *absolution* altogether—at least, till the Day of Judgment

"At a later period the Church became more courtly, if not more loving , discipline began to fall away , and a priestly official, called a *Penitentiary*, was allowed, in lieu of sharper

---

* 1 Cor. v 15 , 2 Cor ii 5–11.
† *Vide* Bingham's "Antiquities."

measures, to receive *private confessions* at the sinner's mouth, and thereupon to give him *absolution.* But a great scandal having occurred in Constantinople, involving the character of a lady, the office was summarily abolished, and 'the Catholic doctrine of confession' lay at loose ends for a time.

"Afterward, the Latin Church stiffened by degrees, amid a great flood of scandals, into its present way of accounting all alike to be sinners, and of enforcing confession and absolution upon *all* as a *sine qua non* of communion.

"The Greek Church settled into a practice much the same, save that in the East, confession being made to married priests, and each sinner being restricted to his own pastor, there is less coarseness in the examination of penitents, less of mutual underbidding among the priests, less jealousy and wrangling, less disturbance of the peace of families, less casuistry, less mystery, and altogether less scandal and confusion, than in the rival communion. So, at least, I have heard from an eminent and intelligent Greek priest. It is a mistake to suppose, however, that confession is less obligatory among the Greeks than among the Latins. No man comes to the communion without notice to his priest, or without some examination of conscience—though this examination is for the most part summary, and has nothing of the formality of what is called 'Auricular Confession,' and, in fact, is a different sort of thing.

"In the Anglican Church the old distinction is maintained between an ordinary Christian and a 'notorious evil liver,' the latter term including any one known to have wronged his neighbor by word or deed, or even any one betwixt whom and any other 'the *minister* perceiveth malice and hatred to reign.' Such an one must openly declare himself to have truly repented and amended his former evil life, 'to the satisfaction of the minister and the congregation,' who, being satisfied, the minister ought to admit 'the penitent person to the Holy Communion, and not him that is obstinate' This, of course, cannot be done without at least virtual confession and absolution, the priest meanwhile holding the offender in a state of practical excommunication, from which only himself or the Ordinary can release him. Thus 'enforced confession' is the rule of the Church, restricted, however, as in the early Church, to notorious evil livers, and to sins which cause scandal, hatred, and the like

"With regard to the large class who come not under this category, but who yet are more or less conscious of sin, the Church enjoins, in the first place, thorough self-examination, bewailing of sin, confession to God, full purpose of amendment, restitution, satisfaction, forgiveness ; and, in the second place, if there is still a lack of full trust in God's mercy, or of a quiet conscience, or of further comfort or counsel, she sends the sinner to the pastor, or to some other minister, that he may open his grief, and *'that he may receive the benefit of absolution.'* I quote these last words from the English book, because I am now speaking only of the Anglican Church's doctrine on the subject, which is of course the same in both books, our American Church having solemnly declared, in her *Preface,* that in the verbal variations she has made, she is far from intending to depart from the Church of England in any essential point of doctrine, discipline, or worship, or further than local circumstances require

"This doctrine I freely confess myself to have held during all my ministerial life. Moreover, so far as the care of my own soul is concerned, I have practised what I hold ; though, from a fear of misapprehension and want of zeal, I have been far too infrequent in the use of this help, as well as too slack in recommending so salutary a medicine to others Yet, in cases not a few, some of them clergymen, my superiors in age, piety, and zeal, I have felt obliged to do for others what I have known to be good for myself As a matter of taste, however, I do not always call the thing 'confession,' much less by such a sounding name as 'Catholic confession,' but am content to regard it as a conference, a *confidential* talk on spiritual matters. At the present day religion is choking itself with *names*. If people would look more at things, and less at words, the Church would be far better off.

"And in all this, I think I differ little, if at all, from the practical belief of the clergy generally, of all sects and parties and views. There is a well-grounded dislike of such terms as 'auricular confession,' 'Popish confession,' 'confession to man,' and the like; and I must say, in passing, that where Mr Gray uses the expression, 'confession to man,' and defends it, I think he might have employed a better phrase, though his meaning is safe enough; for when the Church exhorts a person to come to *me* or to some other discreet and learned minister of God's Word, I do not understand her to mean *me* or any other minister as a *mere man*, but rather as an *ambassador for Christ*, and 'as though God did beseech you *by us*,' while 'we pray you in *Christ's stead*, be ye reconciled to God.' True confession is always to God, however much the instrumentality of man may be used, for comfort, counsel, and the like; and true '*absolution*' comes only from God, by whatever messenger, or in whatever form, it may be conveyed. But saving some objection to phrases, capable of misinterpretation, or at least of exception, I believe religious men of all sects and parties would be glad to see a greater readiness on the part of clergy and laity alike to confide their spiritual griefs to some 'learned and discreet minister,' who should feel himself under bonds, as it were, to know nothing of men's secrets *as a man*, but only as God's angel, ministering in the presence of God.

"There is a feeling among us all, that if we could *know* our people better, our people would know us. But to know any one really, in spiritual affairs, is a rarer thing by far than is commonly imagined. However frank we may be in every-day intercourse, no person ever carries his *soul* upon his sleeve, and if any one should be found who is an exception to this rule in ordinary cases, even he will take care to have an oversleeve for Sundays, or for pastoral visitations On the other hand, few persons would object to frank and frequent conference with the clergy, if only it be done medicinally, and with proper care Hence, all that the clergy need is opportunity and reasonable confidence If they could see their flocks separately, in proper time and place for religious intercourse, if they could learn their griefs, scruples, struggles, weights, besetments, and the like, if they could deal with sins as physicians deal with diseases, not as monsters to make wry faces at, but as infirmities to be healed, the pastoral relation would be much more satisfactory to all parties

"As things go now, society is to the clergy as the woman of Samaria to our Lord What she desires is a pleasant little chat about religion in general—a charming little discussion about Jerusalem and the mountain What He has in view is, a word of solid counsel in relation to her five husbands She wishes to hear *where* men ought to worship He would rather tell her *how she* ought to worship So society bluffs off her spiritual guides, sitting down with them most amiably at any Jacob's well of wayside conversation, and ready to listen eagerly to 'accurate' distinctions of doctrines, 'Catholic' or 'Roman ' but when it comes to the point, as we say—when we ask what *Catholic* 'confession' is, and *where* it is to be found, and *when* and *where* and *how* it is taught and practised—the matter is apt to end less profitably, I fear, than with the woman of Samaria, for she had too firm an eye upon her to be able to escape in that way But society evades us by any colored rag she may flaunt in our faces, and the real religious question of the day, namely, *how to get at our people, how to bring about a real pastoral relation*, is swallowed up in controversies about forms and clothes

"I grant that there is a real difficulty in pushing points of this kind. Clothes or rags are easily converted into scarecrows, and scarecrows, of course, are calculated to scare On the other hand, I submit, they are meant to scare *crows*, not men : so that while there is among us a well-grounded dislike of such terms as 'confession,' or 'confession to man,' yet, I think, we are reasonable creatures, and are bound to deal with mere words in a liberal way Thus, the term 'confession' I do not altogether like, on account of some of its associations ; but it expresses that opening of one's griefs which the Church expressly sanctions, and is sufficiently Catholic in its use to be easily understood 'Auricular' confession is in a different category, because custom associates it only with a particular mode of confession, which is peculiar to Rome

"A greater trust in one another, and more readiness to confess to one another, is a thing which may exist without Rome . and if it may, I think we are all agreed that it ought.

"From this brief sketch we may deduce, at least, the main points of the Catholic doctrine of confession, viz , those points which have been held by all such churches, ancient and modern, as profess to believe in the Holy Catholic Church

"I take them to be, *first*, for open, notorious, scandalous sins, *excommunication, enforced confession*, in connection with such discipline as changing times and places may determine , *absolution*, in such forms and ways as from time to time may be adopted ; entire *restoration* to Church communion With regard to this order, however, and in the same way in regard to any particular forms, words, or ceremonies, or the like, I think the Catholic doctrine to be eminently grounded on the 'law of liberty ' When our Lord said to the paralytic, *rise and walk*, it was all the same, virtually, as to say, ' *Thy sins be forgiven thee* ' When a modern priest says to a sinner, *I admit you to the Lord's Table*, he absolves him as effectually, though not as solemnly, as when an ancient priest laid his hands on him with all the elaborate ceremonial of primitive Catholic times.

" But, *secondly*, for sins not notorious, scandalous, or uncharitable, *private confession* is allowed or commended, but not forced on any man's conscience. It is a part of one's Christian liberty. And where it has come to be enforced, as by the modern Roman Church, it is generally grounded on no doctrine, so far as I understand , but, like the withholding of the cup from the laity, or the celibacy of the clergy, or kneeling at the Communion, or numberless other things of the sort, it is simply a matter of disciplinary law, a matter of wise—or unwise—legislation

"Where the Latin or Greek Church imposes confession upon all alike, it is done by special legislation, as a matter of discipline, which, like the withholding of the cup from the laity, or denial of marriage to the clergy, is defended on grounds of expediency, or necessity, not of doctrine in the full sense of the word. The Church of England, if she liked, might, on the same grounds, *forbid* private confession altogether. But as she has never done so—as she has never put such an absurd restriction upon the liberty of her children, but allows every one 'to open his griefs' to a minister as freely as he opens his mouth, and to receive his absolution as freely as he receives his 'counsel'—we can appeal to her formularies as sufficiently accurate with regard to the Catholic doctrine of confession

"In short, my doctrine is, with regard to this matter, that a communicant *may*, and, under certain circumstances, ought, to come to some suitable minister, that he may 'open his grief,' which I take to be virtually 'confession ,' and that having thus confessed so as to satisfy his minister of the sincerity of his repentance, he may receive, and the minister ought to grant, 'the benefit of absolution ' This is the length and breadth of my belief or doctrine on the subject

"To all, whatever may be their name or sect, who will give me a fair hearing before they judge, I commend the following *tract ;* not, of course, as an authority in itself, or as a thing that I indorse in every phrase, but as a clear and honest statement of Anglican standards on the subject involved, and as showing that good men of all professions and schools have substantially borne the same witness

"If this is not enough, I respectfully invoke all who are yet dissatisfied to explain to the Church, What is the Catholic doctrine of confession? What the Roman? What the Anglican? What the points of difference among the three, and wherein I am held to differ from all or either? It is surely time to be done with child's play—this mere game of 'bluff' in matters of religious faith Let our opponents come out like men, and tell us, not what to dodge, but what to believe Let us turn over a new leaf, beginning with this deeply interesting subject of confession and absolution Let us learn what our Church teaches, and if she teaches amiss, let us honestly confess it."

Mr. Gray gives, in support of his thesis, the following names:

INDEX TO QUOTATIONS.

First Exhortation to Holy Communion	Second Book of Homilies.
Office for Visitation of Sick	Parker's Visitation Articles.
113th Canon	The Eleven Articles.
Luther	Bacon
Hooker on Lutherans.	Hooker
Melanchthon	King James I
Calvin	Williams.
Cranmer.	Reynolds
The Catechism.	Hakewill
First Prayer Book.	Aylmer.
Ridley	Crakanthorp.
Latimer.	Andrewes
Turner	Donne.
Jewel.	Baily.
	Downame.

APPENDED NOTES 239

Mede.
Montague
Visitation Articles, Overall, etc
Hammond.
Heylin.
Laud
Bramhall
19th Irish Canon.
Ussher
Herbert
N Farrar
Chillingworth
James, Earl of Derby.
Hall
Lady Capel
Lady Anderson.
Morton
Jeremy Taylor.
Sanderson
Pierce
Thorndike
Nicholson.
Cosin.
Mr Adams' Sermon.
Grenville
Barrow
Evelyn's Diary.
Sparrow
Puller
Comber

Pearson
Fourteen Bishops on case of Friend and Parkins.
Patrick
Dodwell
Isham.
Beveridge.
Ken
Bull
Sharpe.
Hickes
Nicholls
Marshall.
Hole
Fiddes.
Wake
Secker
Berkeley.
Wheatley.
Wilson
Horne
Tomline.
Marsh
Short
Hamilton.
Mobeily
Confessor in King's Household
Keble (Note A).
Baxter (Note B).

www.ingramcontent.com/pod-product-compliance
Lightning Source LLC
Chambersburg PA
CBHW062012220426
43662CB00010B/1302